101

QUESTIONS AND ANSWERS

ON

Buddhism

Also by the author

101 Questions and Answers on Islam
101 Questions and Answers on Hinduism

101

QUESTIONS AND ANSWERS

ON

Buddhism

John Renard

GRAMERCY BOOKS
New York

This 2002 edition is published by Gramercy Books, an imprint of
Random House Value Publishing, Inc., 280 Park Avenue, New York,
NY 10017, by arrangement with Paulist Press.

Gramercy is a registered trademark and the colophon is a
trademark of Random House, Inc.

Random House
New York • Toronto • London • Sydney • Auckland
www.randomhouse.com

Printed and bound in the United States of America

[Previously published as *Responses to 101 Questions on Buddhism*.]

A catalog record for this title is available from the
Library of Congress.

ISBN 0-517-22082-2

10 9 8 7 6 5 4 3 2 1

To our nieces and nephews
Katie, Sarah, and Mimi
Michael and Mark
Louis, Fran, and Raphael
Patrick, Mary Kate, Jack and John
Sarah, Erin, J.T.
Seamus, and Bridget Rose
Miroku's Children All

CONTENTS

PREFACE

As the third volume in a matched set, this book is arranged in nine sections to parallel the structure of its companion volumes on Islam and Hinduism. The first two sections give historical background about the beginnings and spread of Buddhism, along with explicit attention to the various ranges of Buddhist sacred scripture. Sections three through five deal with a host of matters relating to doctrine, ritual, legal and ethical problems, and spirituality. Part six explores the ways in which the Buddhist tradition has contributed to developing, and communicated through, the various fields of humanistic learning and the arts. Section seven discusses Buddhism's manifold relationships with various other traditions, beginning with those with which it connected most immediately in its Indian context (Hinduism and Jainism) and then moving to others with which Buddhism came into contact as it traveled (Confucianism, Taoism, Shinto, and Christianity). Section eight is dedicated to matters especially pertinent to women, family, and gender. Finally, various items of more recent or contemporary interest fill part nine. In the interest of simplicity, I have opted for a type of minimalist transliteration intended to help toward something at least approaching correct pronunciation; in the case of technical terms of Indic origin, I refer only to the Sanskrit rather than to the Pali equivalents. Unless explicitly indicated B.C.E., all dates are C.E.

My gratitude goes especially to the Jesuit community of Sophia University in Tokyo, to Sophia's Institute of Asian Cultures, to the Sisters of Notre Dame College in Kyoto, to the Jesuit Community of Sogang University in Seoul, and to the T'ien Jesuit Educational Center in Taipei, for the opportunities my visits there in 1983 and 1985 afforded for coming into closer contact with living Buddhism. Thanks also to the College

ix

of Arts and Sciences of Saint Louis University for the additional time to write provided by the Eugene Hotfelder Professorship in the Humanities and to the countless anonymous scholars of Buddhism whose work appears here under the guise of this stranger's words. In a more personal vein, I thank those scholars of various aspects of Buddhism—Roger Corless, Heinrich Dumoulin, Paul Griffiths, Masatoshi Nakatomi, John Rosenfield, David Snellgrove—whose lectures, publications, and collegial conversation over the years have put a face on the subject. My special thanks go to James Fredericks of Loyola-Marymount University in Los Angeles for his helpful suggestions after reading an early draft. To David Vila and Mindi Grieser of Saint Louis University, I am particularly grateful for their research and editorial assistance, especially in proofreading and indexing the volume. Special thanks also to David Vila for providing the charts and tables. Finally, as always, thanks to my own Miroku, wife Mary Pat.

LIST OF QUESTIONS ON BUDDHISM

One: Beginnings and Early Sources

1. How did you become interested in Buddhism? Why should I care about Buddhism?
2. Where and in what circumstances did Buddhism begin?
3. Who was the Buddha, and what do we know of his life?
4. What do Buddhists consider the principal moments of the Buddha's life?
5. What kind of community or social structure did Buddhism develop? Did the Buddha have "disciples" as Jesus did? What was their role?
6. Did any variant interpretations of the Buddha and his teaching develop in the early centuries?
7. Did the Buddha himself write or dictate a sacred text?
8. Did any of the other early schools develop their own scriptural canons as did the Theravadins?
9. How did Buddhism manage to survive and grow so dramatically during that half-millennium after the Buddha?
10. Is there any significant archaeological data on early Buddhism? What story does that physical evidence tell?

Two: History and Development

11. What role has monasticism played in the development and spread of Buddhism?
12. Apart from the reigns of Ashoka and Kanishka, has Buddhism ever been associated directly with political structures or regimes?

Three: Doctrines and Practices

Buddhism holds that the Buddha was more than a historical figure, did it evolve a way to describe his ongoing spiritual significance?

31. Because they consider the Buddha a historical teacher rather than a spiritual presence, do Theravada Buddhists have regular ritual practices? Are Mahayana rituals significantly different?
32. Is there a Buddhist liturgical calendar? What are some of the principal Buddhist religious observances?
33. Statues of the Buddha so often depict him in meditation. Is meditation an important practice for Buddhists?
34. Has pilgrimage been an important practice for Buddhists?

Four: Law and Ethics

35. Is there anything like a central teaching authority for Buddhists? Are there significant ethical differences among the various schools?
36. Is there a characteristically Buddhist moral virtue?
37. Is there also a more practical side to Buddhist ethics that helps one decide how to put compassion into action?
38. The "Wheel of the Law" with its eight spokes seems to be an important image for Buddhists. Why so?
39. We hear a lot of talk these days about various "syndromes" allegedly responsible for the criminal actions of some individuals. What does Buddhism have to say about that sort of thing?
40. If Buddhists believe there is "no-self" behind the appearances of individuality, how can they talk about individual ethical responsibility?
41. What is the connection between Buddhist ethics and salvation? Is there a faith–works controversy? Do Buddhists have anything similar to the concepts of *predestination* or the *will of God?*
42. How does evil manifest itself, according to Buddhist thought? Is there anything like a devil or demons?
43. Are there specific ethical expectations for monks and for lay people?

60. How did Buddhist visual arts develop their iconographic themes, and how do they function in Buddhist life?
61. What are some of the other important iconographic themes in Buddhist art?
62. Have there been any especially important Buddhist painters? Can one detect a distinctively Buddhist aesthetic in their work?
63. I've seen numerous statues of the Buddha in museums. How important is religious sculpture in Buddhism? Are there rules for crafting these images?
64. Does music play a significant role in Buddhist religious life?
65. Have Buddhists cultivated creative forms of literature as vehicles for religious thought?
66. Have dance, drama, or other performance arts been important in Buddhist religious ritual or entertainment?

Seven: Relationships to Other Religious Traditions

67. How would you describe Buddhism's relationship to Hinduism?
68. What are some significant features of Buddhism's relationship to Jainism?
69. What are some of the main features of Buddhism's relationship to Confucianism?
70. What about Buddhism's relationship with the Chinese indigenous tradition called Daoism?
71. How did Buddhism interact with Shinto, Japan's indigenous tradition? Was the process of inculturation in Japan anything like "dialogue"?
72. Did the Second Vatican Council make any statements about the Catholic Church's official view of Buddhism?
73. What are some of the major differences between Buddhist and Christian doctrinal systems?
74. What are some areas of potentially fruitful dialogue between Buddhists and Christians? Why is this important now?
75. What was Thomas Merton's connection with Buddhism?
76. Is the phenomenon of monasticism a significant link between Christianity and Buddhism?

Eight: Women and Family

77. Can women achieve enlightenment and salvation? Can they become Buddhas?
78. What role have nuns played in Buddhist life? Are there significant differences in monastic rules for monks and for nuns?
79. You mentioned at one point that Buddhist monks are ordained. Is there a ceremony like that for women who become nuns? Does it have anything like the significance it has in some Christian traditions?
80. I've heard the sacred figure named Kwan Yin in China referred to as "the Goddess of Mercy." Could you explain that?
81. Are there other "goddesses" in Buddhist belief?
82. I remember hearing in a Bible study course years ago that the figure of Wisdom in the Hebrew scripture was feminine. Are there any parallels in Buddhism?
83. Buddhist iconography features some fearsome-looking male figures. Are there similarly fearsome females?
84. The Buddha and other famous teachers have stood as role models of a sort for young Buddhist men; are there similar religious role models for young women?
85. On a visit to Japan, we saw several temples where people had gathered hundreds of small statues with little red knit caps and children's pinwheels. What is that about?
86. Is "holy-family imagery" important in Buddhist piety as it is, say, in Christian and Hindu traditions?
87. Are there distinctive Buddhist rituals and views around marriage? What about divorce?
88. What do the classic Buddhist sources say about "family values"?
89. Birth seems to be a major element in the Buddhist notion of suffering. Is birth a cause for blaming women? Is there rejoicing in a Buddhist family when a child is born?

Nine: Buddhism Here and Now

BUDDHISM TIMELINE

c. 563–483 B.C.E.	Life of the Buddha
473	First Buddhist Council
383	Second Buddhist Council
273–236	Reign of Ashoka
250	Third Buddhist Council
c. 200	Rise of Mahayana Buddhism; Theravada Buddhism
160	Prajna-paramita Literature
120	Synod of the Sarvastivadins
c. 100	Lotus Sutra; Pali Canon
r. 120–162 C.E.	Emperor Kanishka
c. 150	Fourth Buddhist Council
c. 200	Nagarjuna, philosopher
220–552	Missions to Vietnam, China, Korea, Burma, Java, Sumatra, Japan
fl. c. 430	Buddhaghosa, philosopher
594	Buddhism proclaimed Japanese state religion
749	First Buddhist monastery in Tibet
800	Founding of Japanese Tendai (Saicho d. 822) and Shingon (Kukai d. 835) schools
845	T'ang Dynasty persecutes Chinese Buddhists
1065	Hindu Invasion of Sri Lanka
1133–1212	Honen; Japanese Pure Land
1193–1227	Rise of Japanese Zen lineages
1203	Destruction of Vikramasila, end of Buddhism in India

1222–1282	Nichiren, philosopher
1260–1368	Tibetan Buddhism influential in China
1360	Buddhism becomes state religion in Thailand
1543–1588	Final conversion of Mongols
1856–1857	Fifth Buddhist Council
1868–1871	Meiji Persecution of Buddhism in Japan
1954–1956	Sixth Buddhist Council in Rangoon, Burma
1959	Communist China represses Buddhism in Tibet

ONE:

BEGINNINGS AND EARLY SOURCES

1. How did you become interested in Buddhism? Why should I care about Buddhism?

What do pop star Tina Turner and former Chicago Bulls Coach Phil Jackson have in common? They and a surprising number of other famous Americans have discovered the mysteries of Buddhism. She finds peace in chanting, and he uses Zen techniques to help him focus. But, you might ask, why should I bother to learn about something that still seems pretty exotic? First, because Buddhism is slowly but surely becoming a part of the American religious scene; second, because we have here one way to move toward understanding the fascinating cultures of East and Southeast Asia in which Buddhism has been a major presence for two millennia; and third, because appreciating the vast spiritual heritage of Buddhism can enrich one's own spiritual life.

Buddhism is not the oldest of the world's major religious traditions—that distinction belongs, arguably, to either Hinduism or Judaism—nor, at around five hundred million adherents, is it the biggest—Christianity still leads in that category, followed a close second by Islam. But through the elegance and power of its various systems of thought and schools of art, Buddhism has exerted a profound and enduring influence in so many Asian cultures. It is therefore all the more critical that those of us whose worldview is so often limited to Europe and the Americas open our minds to the marvel and mystery of "The Middle Path."

In 1968 I began work as a teacher. The previous year I had taken a course that included Buddhism as one of its main components, and my first teaching assignment was to make Buddhism and the other major religious traditions as engaging to high school juniors as it was to me. During the ensuing 30 years I continued to teach secondary, college, and adult education courses in the history and art of the world's Buddhist, Hindu, and Muslim faith communities. Impressed early on with what seemed consistently negative coverage of Islam both in the news media and in teaching materials, I decided to focus my efforts on doctoral work in Islamic Studies. But through the years I have remained intrigued by the Buddhist tradition and concerned that so few of the academic institutions

3

in which I have taught or studied have devoted even minimal attention to educating their students about the lands of Buddhism's origins and ongoing influence, chiefly, India, China, Korea, Japan, and the nations of Southeast Asia.

Squeezing in courses and institutes on Buddhism and related subjects when possible during summers and as a sideline during graduate studies, I have had the additional luxury of some extended travel in Asia. During several months in summer 1983 and again in winter 1985, I devoted much of my time to visiting Buddhist temples and monasteries and to studying the art of the tradition, both activities in Japan, Korea, and Taiwan. A stint as a faculty member on the University of Pittsburgh's Semester at Sea program in fall 1988 added a third brief stop in Japan, a second in Taiwan, and new experiences of the People's Republic of China and Malaysia.

Buddhism is in some ways the most inviting and hospitable religious tradition I have had the privilege of studying. Kyoto's Zenrinji temple extended its own invitation to me 15 years ago. According to legend, a monk named Eikan came early one day to pray in the shrine room. As he stood reciting from scripture, the Buddha came down to join the monk. Standing just in front of Eikan and turning to face the altar, the Buddha looked to his left and gestured to Eikan with his left hand to come forward and pray with him. On the altar of that temple, now called Eikando in honor of the monk, a unique statue of the Buddha commemorates the encounter, recalling that there is after all a reality beyond even the Enlightened One that both he and the seeker must acknowledge. Ever since that day at the Eikando, I have been increasingly aware of an invitation to continue looking through Buddhism to the reality beyond; I hope this book will offer readers the same kind of invitation.

2. Where and in what circumstances did Buddhism begin?

Between about 800 B.C.E. and 500 B.C.E., Indian societies witnessed growing dissatisfaction with the ritualism of ancient Vedic religion. Prominent during the earliest period of Hindu history, Vedic religion centered on the original scriptures, the four Vedas, and was under tight control of the priestly class, known as Brahmins. Nonconformist groups became more vocal in their criticism, feudal breakdown gradually transferred power to the warrior class, and the Brahmanical monopoly began to crumble. New forms of religious literature, the Upanishads in particular, reflected the social ferment. Religious seekers began to look inward for answers to life's great questions, refining their understanding of the human person. No longer merely a puppet of capricious gods, the individual was emerging as a center of consciousness, knowledge replacing ritual precision as the path to meaning. Eventually mainstream religious specialists found a way to integrate the new thinking by interpreting Hindu tradition as a dual system embracing both action and knowledge as means of salvation.

But some segments of Indian society remained unconvinced, rejecting even the Upanishads in the belief that they failed to address the deepest questions of human existence and spirituality. Reform-minded seekers began to articulate the psychological implications of the ancient concepts. They redefined action *(karma)* so that it meant not only external ritual but inward choices; reinterpreted the notion of endless cycles of rebirth *(samsara)* so that it included interior states through which one passed en route to knowledge; and personalized the concept of cosmic law *(dharma)* so that it related directly to the individual as moral agent.

Most of these splinter groups organized their conviction of the relative spiritual autonomy of each person around the notion of an indestructible self or soul *(atman)* that survives each physical death, returning to be reembodied until at last it gains release *(moksha)*. Some, however, regarded even the idea of immortal soul as a potential distraction from the ultimate goal of the religious quest. In a radical departure, these "naysayers" *(nastikas,* "those who say it does not exist") included the Buddha (c. 563–483 B.C.E.) and his early followers. Acceptance of *atman* became a sort of litmus test of Hindu orthodoxy, and the Buddhists failed. Belief in such an indestructible personal core, they argued, was a form of spiritual narcissism that offered only a false sense of security.

These and other developments constitute Buddhism's most challenging contributions to a period in world history that some have called an Axial Age. Important developments in knowledge and belief usually evolve out of broader, often indefinable undercurrents of culture. Some periods in human history appear, in the foreshortened perspective of telephoto hindsight, to have seen especially dramatic change in the way we human beings have viewed ourselves and our world. Not only in India but elsewhere as well, societies witnessed earth-shaking revolutions in religious, social, and political structures. Greek philosophy and the dawning of Mediterranean democracy, the incisive moral commentary of Israel's pre-exilic prophets, the teaching of Zoroaster in Iran, the beginnings of Confucianism in China, and major reinterpretations of the Hindu tradition in India are among the most striking and far-reaching hallmarks of the age. Buddhism, along with the much smaller and still largely Indian tradition called Jainism, grew out of the last of these great movements.

3. Who was the Buddha, and what do we know of his life?

According to fairly sound historical evidence, Siddhartha ("He who has achieved his goal") Gautama was born around 563 B.C.E. to Maya and Shuddhodana of the ancient warrior *(kshatriya)* tribe called the Shakyas. They lived in the kingdom of Maghada to the northeast of the Ganges River in part of what is now Nepal. We know the general out-lines of his life, but much of the detail is enshrined in legend. Siddhartha's father knew of the imminent birth of his son through a celestial visitation, his mother Maya through a dream. Noting the 36 bodily marks that suggested that the newborn boy would be either a world renouncer *(sannyasin)* or a "wheel turner" *(chakravartin,* Sanskrit for "mover and shaker"), the anxious father sought sage counsel in the hope of ensuring the latter possibility. To insulate the boy from whatever might incline him toward renunciation, the prince sequestered his son behind the palace walls, surrounded with beauty and luxury. Siddhartha married at 16, had a son, and seemed happy enough for a time. But his father's plan failed, and as the young Siddhartha became aware of suffering, he grew disillusioned.

Exactly what sad events drove him away from home we do not know for certain, but tradition preserves a formulaic account called the story of the "four passing sights." It recounts how on successive forays outside the palace confines, the young Siddhartha came of age. As the prince's servants failed to remove every reminder of the hard side of the human condition, the young man saw a decrepit individual and inquired what the matter was. Old age, the servants said. About a leper in agony he asked; sickness, they replied. About a procession of mourners; they told him about death. But who, he asked, is that young man who seems content and serene though he obviously possesses nothing? That, they answered, is a world renouncer. The prince redoubled his efforts to keep Siddhartha pleasure-bound, but he was about to lose his 29-year-old son.

Siddhartha knew that hedonism could not satisfy him. Now his quest took him to a succession of Hindu gurus and Jain ascetics. After six years, he set off on his own, persuaded that the Hindu focus on the self and the Jain emphasis on dire austerity led nowhere. At age 35, the wanderer found himself meditating under a tree. For seven weeks, he sought insight there near the village of Gaya, passing through four trancelike stages until at last he arrived at an absolute personal freedom and detachment in which the extremes of fear and hope, pain and pleasure loosened their grip on him. Knowledge of the startlingly simple liberating truth earned Siddhartha the title of the Enlightened One, the Buddha. Part of the struggle for enlightenment meant fighting off the temptation to keep the fruits of his quest for himself. He overcame that, formed a community of followers, and spent the next 45 years passing the message on to others. Around 483 B.C.E., the Buddha died, of food poisoning some say, in the town of Kushinagara, under a tree. Thus ended the 80-year earthly life of the man sometimes called Shakyamuni, the "Sage of the Shakya" clan.

4. What do Buddhists consider the principal moments of the Buddha's life?

Buddhist tradition includes a "canonical" collection of Buddha's 547 previous lives as the Buddha-to-be, as well a group of major events in the founder's life. Among the 547 *Jatakas* ("Birth Stories") that tell of the previous lives of the Buddha there is a de facto hierarchy. Each of the stories recounts how the bodhisattva (enlightenment being) entered the world of human affairs in a different form, many animal and some human, to work his saving compassion among the suffering. But the last 10 of the tales have come to form an integral set, often depicted in manuscript and mural painting, on which devotees can meditate. Each story exemplifies one essential moral virtue that every Buddhist ought to cultivate, and the Buddha's keen awareness and recollection of all his previous lives is itself a model for all who seek enlightenment.

The central occurrences in the life of the historical Buddha Shakyamuni function in the liturgical calendar, ritual, and devotional iconography somewhat the way, for example, the "12 feasts" of Christ do in Orthodox Christianity. Buddhists speak of "eight episodes," of which four events form a primary grouping that are universally accepted, while the remaining four are drawn from a list that includes several variants. The history of Buddhist art is on the whole a visual record of these key events, with numerous other images besides. First come the events surrounding the Buddha's birth and infancy. Tradition says that after Buddha descended from Tushita heaven, he was born from his mother's side. He then immediately took seven steps to the north and proclaimed himself exalted and free from rebirth. Naturally the four "passing sights" figure prominently, and then the "Great Renunciation" in which Siddhartha is carried aloft beyond the palace walls on a cloud-borne steed. Other episodes include several lesser miraculous deeds.

In the middle of it all is the experience of meditation and enlightenment, often captured in images of the "earth touching" gesture in which the Buddha, after overcoming the temptations of the evil demon Mara, summons the earth to quell Mara's minions. (Other versions say that Mara accuses Buddha of impure motives in his quest for enlightenment, or that the god Indra implores the Buddha to teach rather than withdraw into solitude, whereupon he calls the earth to witness the rightness of his choice.) Meeting shortly thereafter with a group of five of his former fellow-ascetics at Sarnath north of Banaras, Buddha preached his inaugural sermon. Called the Turning of the Wheel of the Law sermon, his message recalls how dearly his father had wanted his son to be a "wheel turner." Buddha's bodily demise coincides with the "Great Ultimate Nirvana" (Mahaparinirvana) that brought to completion the reality which Buddha had attained at initial enlightenment, namely, nirvana, the cessation of desire. He had achieved nirvana prior to his death, but with the dissolution of his corporeal existence, he entered into nirvana "without a remainder." Buddha's birth, enlightenment, wheel-turning sermon, and final nirvana are often associated with the cardinal directions: east/sunrise, south/solar zenith, west/sunset, and north/solar nadir, respectively.

5. What kind of community or social structure did Buddhism develop? Did the Buddha have "disciples" as Jesus did? What was their role?

A Tokyo temple dedicated to the "Five Hundred Disciples" of the Buddha (Gohyaku Rakanji) enshrines what remains of an original grouping of 500 nearly life-size wooden statues, each of a different likeness as if to represent actual followers. It is a strange, almost eerie sight, but it brought home to me for the first time something of the concrete reality of the earliest Buddhist community, the *sangha* ("together-going, assembly"). The little audience in attendance at the first sermons the Buddha preached would become the first monks and lay disciples, members of what is perhaps history's oldest continuously functioning human institution. From very early times, a group of basic precepts regulated the life of the *sangha*. Some applied to lay persons as well as to monks and nuns: refraining from violence, stealing, deception, intoxicants, and adultery. Rules governing moderate consumption of food and doing without cosmetics, "broad or high beds," and gold or silver applied only to monks and nuns.

Early Buddhist monks wore saffron robes and begged for their food and clothing. Pious benefactors received the gift of the Buddha's teaching *(dharma)* in return. Though they regarded a life of mobile mendicancy as the ideal, regular and protracted monsoon seasons forced them to settle in for several months of the year. At first they resisted being attached to permanent rainyseason residences, but as devotees donated more land and facilities, they began to maintain established monasteries to which they would return during monsoon. Gradually their periods of residence in the monastery lengthened, and a regular order of monastic life evolved. Monks lived in separate cells but came together for various activities. The members devoted themselves to regular recitation of the rules of discipline that they had committed to memory. They observed a day of fast and abstinence every fortnight, at new and full moons in Hindu style, eating the second of their two regular daily meals at noon so as to devote the rest of the day to meditation. Every two weeks, they would engage in a public confession of transgressions. During Buddha's lifetime, members were allowed to express good-faith dissent, have the community vote on the opinion, and then even go off to form a new branch of the sangha with the teacher's blessing. Eventually the community evolved a structure of ranks and stages of spiritual attainment, from the least committed lay person to the most advanced elder monk.

From the start, an important spiritual reciprocity has bound monks *(bhikshu,* from the root *bhik,* related to the English "beg") and lay persons *(upasaka)* together. According to the concept of religious mutuality, the lay person gives material needs, and the monk or nun's grateful acceptance returns religious merit to the donor, thus assisting him or her toward enlightenment. Lay and monastic Buddhists base their respective roles on those of the Buddha, who was both the teacher engaged in the world and the mendicant who withdrew to meditate. Unlike Jesus, the Buddha seems to have practiced a specific ritual of ordination to monkhood. Also unlike Jesus, Buddha had a very long public ministry, 45 years during which many disciples attached themselves to the teacher, making the 500 (a figure mentioned in an early scripture) of the Tokyo temple, a nice round number indicating " a lot." Of those 500, tradition gradually focused on 10 specific disciples as paragons of particular virtues, such as asceticism, wisdom, knowledge of the Law, monastic discipline, and even esoteric practices. But the Buddha does not appear to have deliberately formed a select group of disciples analogous to the 12 apostles of Jesus.

6. Did any variant interpretations of the Buddha and his teaching develop in the early centuries?

Differences of opinion and variant interpretations of the Buddha's life and teaching began even while the founder lived, and significant divisions began to emerge very soon after his *parinirvana*. The first major points of contention centered around the nature of authority and whether the *sangha* would truly embrace lay persons as well as monks. On the one hand, the Buddha had counseled his followers to be lamps unto their own feet, holding up the self-sufficient *arhat* (senior monk, community elder) as a spiritual ideal; on the other, he had clearly put great emphasis on the importance of community.

An *arhat* named Kashyapa was grief-stricken at Buddha's *parinirvana,* for the living guide was gone; another named Subbadhra said that he now considered himself utterly free and bound only by his own interpretation. Just months after Buddha's *parinirvana,* Kashyapa convened a meeting at Rajagriha a little north of Bodhgaya, in north-central India, the place of Enlightenment. In hopes of combatting Subbadhra's lax attitude, he summoned experts, Ananda (who was not yet an *arhat*) on discipline *(vinaya)* and Upali on doctrine *(dharma).* Ananda reported that the Buddha had freed the community to abrogate minor precepts, but when Ananda admitted that he had failed to ask the teacher to distinguish clearly between minor and major rules, the *arhats* berated him and decided to retain the rule unaltered. The upshot of this first "council" was a widening gap between communitarians and individualists, but the arhats evidently did not wield universal legislative authority, so they could not rule definitively on the matter. They had, however, managed to seize control of the sangha, thus tilting decidedly toward a monastic model and away from the more devotional spirituality that appealed to lay Buddhists.

A hundred years later, in 383 B.C.E., a monk named Vashas convened 700 delegates to a council in the town of Vaishali to discipline wayward local monks who had contemplated accepting money from lay donors. Again the council gave the nod to stricter interpretation and monastic control. Tradition says that this council marked a major schism when the party called the Mahasanghikas ("proponents of the great assembly") challenged the view of a faction of elders called the Sthaviras that an arhat was by spiritual attainment infallible and beyond ordinary human imperfection. This was not a case of theological hairsplitting. At issue here is the question of how far the monastic leaders were willing to go in sharing their spiritual authority. The Mahasanghikas proposed a more inclusive definition of sangha that included lay persons, thus leaving open the possibility that a lay person might achieve the highest of four levels of spiritual attainment, that of an arhat. The Sthaviras held to a more exclusive view, restricting membership in the sangha, and thus access to the status of arhat, to monks. The parties split formally in 367 B.C.E., paving the way for still more momentous schisms. At the Third Council, at Pataliputra in 250 B.C.E., the Sthaviras experienced continued disagreement over metaphysical questions, which led eventually to the formation of several other sects including the Theravada, or Way of the Elders, the most important of the so-called Hinayana ("small vehicle") groups. Meanwhile the Mahasanghikas, with their tendency toward popular devotion, the deification of the Buddha, and a doctrine of salvation that included intermediate spiritual beings called bodhisattvas, were themselves further dividing into at least six subgroups.

7. Did the Buddha himself write or dictate a sacred text?

In the development of its earliest sacred texts, Buddhism shares some features with Christianity, some with Islam. Buddhism is like Christianity in that Buddha himself did not deliberately compose a sacred text either orally or in writing. It is like Islam in that the Buddha's disciples did not get around to writing down the teachings of the founder until some time after his death (although in the case of Islam the primary scripture was committed to writing fairly soon after Muhammad's death and long before the sayings of the Prophet, the Hadith, were written down). For many generations, Buddhist monks kept alive the scripture as oral text, reciting lengthy sections of it from memory in daily communal gatherings where lapses in accuracy could be noted with relative ease during recitation and corrected immediately. Curiously enough, the early Buddhists did not insist on a canonical language, allowing recitation in each person's native dialect.

The earliest and most complete collection is called the Three Baskets (Tripitaka). Connected with the Theravada school, it is also known as The Pali Canon, after the language in which it is composed. Just as the New Testament was written in Greek even though Jesus probably spoke Aramaic, so the initial Buddhist scriptures do not preserve the Buddha's teaching in his own northeast Indian language but in a vernacular language related to Sanskrit. Each of the "baskets" is an anthology of mostly prose texts organized around a large theme, the first a compilation of the rules of monastic discipline *(Vinaya pitaka);* the second a treasury of five collections *(nikaya)* of the Buddha's discourses *(Sutra pitaka);* and the last a set of seven much more theoretical and highly technical scholastic–philosophical interpretations of the Buddha's teaching *(Abhidharma pitaka).*

The first two baskets are considerably older than the third, and it is of interest that the latter was included in the canon even though it was composed by religious scholars from the fourth century B.C.E. on and never purported to be the direct teaching of the Buddha. The first official formulation of the canon occurred at the Third Council, in 250 B.C.E., which formally admitted the *Abhidharma* pitaka as the third major section. All of this the delegates handled through oral transmission, an enormous task to say the least. Tradition records that the scriptures were first committed to writing as a 10,000-page text in around the year 80 B.C.E. in Sri Lanka, but evidence suggests the text is about a century older and from the north of India. Even in these relatively early stages of development, Buddhist sacred texts amounted to a veritable library, and the Pali Canon was only the beginning.

MAJOR BUDDHIST SCRIPTURES

Pali Canon (Tripitaka, "Three Baskets")

Vinaya-Pitaka ("Basket of Order"): contains material about the life of the Buddha and the origin of the monastic community, including the rules of discipline for monks.

Sutra-Pitaka ("Basket of Instruction"): contains teachings of the Buddha and his early disciples and the 547 *Jataka* tales of the Buddha's previous lives.

Abhidharma-Pitaka ("Basket of Higher Teaching"): contains seven sections of teaching designed for specialized instruction of advanced initiates, and dates from the fourth century B.C.E.

Other Buddhist Scriptures

The Mahavastu: Dating from around the first century B.C.E., this text was originally part of a much larger collection produced by the Mahasanghika school. It focuses on the various stages in the career of a Buddha-to-be *(bodhisattva)* and details the various previous lives of the salvific being eventually embodied in the historical Buddha.

Questions of King Milinda (Milindapanha) was compiled in North India around the third century C.E. and is a philosophical dialogue between a Buddhist wise man named Nagasena and the Bactrian king Menander (Pali: Milinda). The discourses cover basic Buddhist themes such as selflessness, suffering, and the attainment of nirvana.

The Lotus of the Good Law Sutra (Saddharmapundarika), used especially by Tendai Buddhists in Japan. This text arose in its present form c. 250 C.E. and is especially concerned with conveying the notion that all sentient beings possess the essential quality necessary for the attainment of Buddhahood.

The Perfection of Wisdom (Prajñaparamita Sutra), parts of which date as far back as the first century C.E., is a collection of sayings of the Buddha that are in effect a comprehensive explanation of the attainment of Buddhahood.

8. Did any of the other early schools develop their own scriptural canons as did the Theravadins?

In addition to the Pali Canon, two others grew out of the early Indian Hinayana schools and one out of Indian Mahayana Buddhism. The Mahasanghika school produced a once-extensive collection of texts originally written in what is called Buddhist hybrid Sanskrit. All has been lost but for the Mahavastu ("The Great Event"), about 2,000 years old, which focuses on the various stages in the career of a Buddha-to-be called a *bodhisattva*. Detailing the various previous lives of the salvific being eventually embodied as the historical Buddha, the text lays the groundwork for the theory of the Buddha's "supramundane" existence that would come to typify later Mahayana teachings about salvation.

One of the more important subsects of the Sthaviras to split off at the Council of Pataliputra in 250 B.C.E. was the Sarvastivada ("Proponents of the View that All Exists"). Their curious metaphysics holds that all things that are, as well as all that have been or will yet come to be, actually exist "now." Like the Mahasanghikas, the Sarvastivadins paved the way for the development of Mahayana thought, especially in their teaching of the six perfections of the bodhisattva, whose upward spiritual progress models the ultimate in virtue. Their scriptural canon was originally written in Sanskrit but has survived almost solely in Chinese and Tibetan translations.

Finally, the first early Indian Mahayana scriptures, also in Sanskrit, developed after the Synod of the Sarvastivadins (a gathering some Buddhists accord the authority of a "general council") in around 120. These texts included three chief types of literature. First were the sutras which claim to be the words of Buddha himself; the most famous are the Lotus of the Good Law Sutra, the Diamond Sutra, and the very brief Heart Sutra. Next are the shastras, typically commentaries on sutras or treatises in philosophical theology, authored by various individuals who signed their names. Last are the tantras, esoteric treatises meant only for initiates in arcane sectarian groups. Many of these works were translated into Chinese, Tibetan, and Japanese during the early centuries C.E.

9. How did Buddhism manage to survive and grow so dramatically during that half-millennium after the Buddha?

But for the support of at least two powerful patrons, Buddhism would probably not have fared so well in India and may not have survived long enough to establish itself beyond India. The Maurya dynasty had come to power in Maghada, land of the Buddha's birth, in 321 B.C.E. From their capital of Pataliputra (present day Patna in the state of Bihar), the Mauryas would gain control over much of northern and central India and continue in power for more than 500 years. To Ashoka, grandson of Chandragupta, founder of the dynasty, fell the task of subduing the last holdout in the region. He conquered Kalinga in 261 B.C.E. but, according to one of his own "rock edicts," was so distraught at the carnage he had wrought that he forsook his Brahmanical Hindu devotion to Shiva to become a Buddhist. Henceforth, the king would make the teaching of the doctrine his sole weapon.

Ashoka declared Buddhism the state creed, proclaiming the universal reign of the dharma in his famous "rock and pillar edicts." He dispatched missionaries throughout India and westward through Afghanistan to the eastern Mediterranean, Egypt, and Greece, as if retracing the route of Alexander's conquest of the previous century. During Ashoka's 40-year reign, Buddhism made greater advances than in all its previous two-and-a-half centuries, but it was still largely confined to the Indian subcontinent. Sri Lanka had responded to Ashokan missionary efforts by becoming and remaining to this day a stronghold of Theravada Buddhism.

Kanishka, a sovereign of the Kushan dynasty, was the next important royal patron of Buddhism and the one whom tradition credits with launching Mahayana Buddhism as a full-fledged missionary faith. Descended from a nomadic tribe that had migrated from China toward present-day Afghanistan in the mid-second century B.C.E., Kanishka ruled c.120–162 from his capital of Peshawar in present-day Pakistan. This latter-day Ashoka, about whom suspiciously similar conversion stories have gathered, lived in a region into which Ashoka himself had introduced missionary Buddhism. He furthered the cause of the faith by convening the Fourth Council, a six-month conclave whose chief product was the beginning of a Sanskrit Mahayana scriptural canon. Under Kanishka, Buddhist sculptors created the earliest-known anthropomorphic images of the Buddha, probably under residual Hellenistic influence; earlier iconography had indicated the Buddha's presence only symbolically, showing a royal parasol, an empty throne, or a pair of footprints.

The degree to which Buddhism mingled with and took on the hues of Hellenistic and Iranian religious beliefs while under Kushan patronage is very hard to assess. But it seems clear that the style of Buddhism

Kanishka sent with his missionaries to China, Tibet, and Burma was of a very different sort from the one Ashoka had sent off to the west nearly 400 years earlier. It is equally clear that by Kanishka's time, Buddhist tradition was branching off into two paths. One, representing what would come to be known as the Hinayana approach, was an arduous climb toward the spiritual perfection of a monastic elite, following the example of a human teacher. The other, representing what would develop into the various Mahayana groups, opened onto a broader and slightly more level road populated by a host of spiritual mediators and leading toward a goal in which all could find themselves in the presence of some compassionate, welcoming manifestation of Enlightenment.

10. Is there any significant archaeological data on early Buddhism? What story does that physical evidence tell?

King Ashoka was the first great builder of monumental Buddhist architecture. Thanks to his patronage, we have a fairly extensive archaeological record of Buddhism beginning slightly more than two centuries after the Buddha's death. Why nothing earlier? Perhaps because the first generations of Buddhists emphasized simplicity of life, used only perishable materials for their communal structures, and chose not to immortalize even their founder with public architectural display. The Buddha was, after all, merely a human being, a great teacher to be sure, but one who habitually deflected the attention of his followers away from himself toward the heart of the spiritual task. That classic view of the function and status of the Buddha had begun to change among some sects, and by Ashoka's time many regarded the Buddha as worthy of devotion as well as reverence.

Among his first projects, Ashoka dedicated colossal earth and masonry reliquary mounds, called *stupas,* at various sites associated with important events in the Buddha's life. A *stupa* is an entirely exteriorized structure consisting of a hemispheric mass (called either the *anda,* "egg," or *garbha,* "womb," containing the "seeds" of the sacred relics). Often raised slightly on a square or circular base, the stupa is surmounted by a square boxy shape, which is in turn crowned with a vertical shaft that supports two, three or five discs *(chattras)* of decreasing diameter. The boxlike form *(harmika),* sometimes surrounded by a stone railing, recalls the enclosed village altar of Vedic Hinduism. The tapered

MAJOR DIFFERENCES BETWEEN MAHAYANA AND THERAVADA BUDDHISM

	Hinayana (including Theravada)	Mahayana
Buddha:	human ethical model	suprahuman savior
Shakyamuni:	historical Buddha	one of innumerable Buddhas
Bodhisattva:	Buddha-to-be (prior lives of Shakyamuni)	intermediary saving figure
Spiritual ideal:	*Arhat,* seeks own enlightenment	*Bodhisattva* seeks to save others
Goal of life:	Nirvana	rebirth in Buddha-land
Means to goal:	meditation, self-discipline	grace of Buddhas and *Bodhisattvas*

disc-bearing pillar is a stylized reminder of both the sacred tree at the center of many villages and the multitiered royal parasols that were long a portable symbol of royalty and authority. The subsequent history of the stupa and its architectural offspring reflect much of the history of Buddhist thought. As Mahayana forms of Buddhism transformed the one historical Buddha from an earthly teacher of the past to an eternal spiritual power of innumerable names and forms, the earth mound gradually melted away and the tree/parasol gained independent existence as the multitiered pagoda.

Although the Buddha had been cremated, many communities claimed to possess various relics, including teeth, some of which Ashoka enshrined in his massive stupas. According to tradition, the king erected 84,000 stupas, each containing a portion of the Buddha's cremated remains. Ashoka's most famous works are stupas at Sanchi, and at Sarnath, where Buddha preached his first sermon. But during the next several centuries, major stupas appeared all over north and central India, resplendent with stone and marble low relief and surrounded by enclosures with monumental gates at the cardinal points. These sites became important goals for pilgrims who would circumambulate the relics, some structures allowing them to ascend to higher levels with each circuit.

Many of the great stupas gradually formed the nucleus of large complexes of ritual and residential structures. As the complexes grew into pilgrimage centers, a liturgical facility known as a *chaitya* took the form of a rectangular hall with a central aisle that led to an apse, and two or more side aisles. The apse housed a smaller version of one of the site's open-air stupas, which devotees circumambulated in processions that encircled the whole structure via the side aisles. Early monastic complexes consisted of rectangular structures called *viharas*, with cells for monks and itinerant ascetics arranged around three sides of an inner courtyard. Early chaityas and viharas were made of wood and have not survived.

At the other end of the architectural spectrum are dozens of almost totally interiorized structures hewn from solid rock like so many sacred caves. Thanks to their permanence, we have a good idea what the wooden chaityas and viharas must have looked like. Between about 300 B.C.E. and 100 C.E., Buddhists carved their chaityas and viharas, at first with no image of the Buddha anywhere, with elaborate facades on the cliff faces of Ajanta, Ellora, and Karli in western India. Mahayana Buddhists transformed formerly Theravada sites by grafting images of the

Stupa (Kathmandu, Nepal).

Buddha onto the stupas and added dozens of their own from the fifth to seventh centuries. As Buddhism waned in India, Hindus and Jains chiseled out their temples along the same cliffs, now become giant sculpture galleries of a millennium of Indian religious history.

TWO:

HISTORY AND DEVELOPMENT

11. What role has monasticism played in the development and spread of Buddhism?

From the earliest days the monastic side of the *sangha* has played a foundational role in Buddhism's growth and continued vitality. Monks and nuns were the first missionaries who were entrusted with spreading the Buddha's teaching not only within India but far beyond. Their evangelistic endeavors began on a modest scale during the Buddha's lifetime and continued for the subsequent two centuries or so within India. Under Ashoka and, to a much greater extent, Kanishka, the role of monastic members as emissaries expanded dramatically. With minimal family responsibilities or none at all, monks and nuns were highly mobile. The earliest mendicant members of the sangha were called "those who go forth," and go forth they did, some as recluses and some as itinerant missionaries. Mahayana Buddhism's emphasis on the role of the bodhisattva as compassionate presence active in the world of ordinary experience increased its orientation to mission. As the sangha diverged into the various "lineages" that took root in diverse new cultural contexts, a variety of missionary styles also developed. But Buddhists everywhere continued to consider the "order" a single universal institution.

Long after monastic communities of the various branches of Mahayana Buddhism had taken the more or less permanent form of stable communities all over east Asia, monks and nuns continued to travel. Now they undertook their journeys for the purpose of acquiring precious texts associated with earlier foundations and teachers. Chinese scholar–monks sought out Sanskrit texts in India. Centuries later, Japanese monks went to China in search of documents and to study Chinese. Such travels sometimes resulted not only in the rediscovery of ancient roots and the reinterpretation of previously known sources but in the creation of whole new movements, devotional styles, and schools of religious art.

As in the history of Christianity, so in that of Buddhism, monks and nuns have often represented a lifeline and a thread of continuity during periods of social and political upheaval. Monastic communities have been the living repository of sacred text that they recite in common.

They have also preserved written versions of the scriptures in their libraries. Members specially trained in calligraphy have shared responsibility for producing faithful new copies. In many times and places, monasteries have been islands of literacy and learning amid swells of barbarism and despair. There too the arts of painting and sculpture have survived during periods of cultural drought. It seems fair to conclude that, all things considered, Buddhism would be little more than a memory had it not been for the monastic sangha.

12. Apart from the reigns of Ashoka and Kanishka, has Buddhism ever been associated directly with political structures or regimes?

Religious traditions rarely grow to the size Buddhism has attained without friends in high places. One of the reasons for Buddhism's decline in India during medieval times was arguably its failure to enjoy continued royal support. During the centuries after Kanishka's considerable patronage, Buddhism was intimately associated with only one of the major Indian dynasties. All the members of the Pala dynasty, which ruled northeast India (Bengal) from about 750 to 1150, professed a type of Buddhism some characterize as an aberrant version of Mahayana in the very heartland of Buddhism's origins. Pala Buddhism was technically a form of Tantra, a blend of mystical and magical elements—spells, chants, and esoteric techniques of visualization—of both Hindu and Buddhist origin.

Meanwhile in faraway Java, the Shailendra dynasty (778–864) represented one of Buddhism's most potent political patrons in the history of Indonesia. Though the dynasty's rule extended to the Malay peninsula and parts of the Indochinese mainland, it is most famous for its building of the great stupa of Barabudur in central Java, one of the world's largest Buddhist monuments. The Shailendras adhered to a variety of Mahayana tradition.

In medieval Cambodia, one of the traditionally Hindu Khmer kings, Jayavarman VII (r.c. 1181–1215) professed Buddhism. In a land that would eventually adopt Theravada Buddhism, Jayavarman leaned toward a form of Mahayana that had been gaining popularity among Khmer subjects for several centuries. He interpreted Buddhism as a metaphysical guarantee of his royal prerogatives and gave it all monumental expression in his royal city Angkor Thom, with images of the Buddha possibly rendered in the sovereign's own likeness. He was not the only ruler who was pleased to identify himself with the Enlightened One.

For a while during early medieval times (eighth to tenth century), Tibet became a Buddhist kingdom of sorts, enjoying the favor of a long line of monarchs. In the long history of Chinese Buddhism, as well, outstanding examples of imperial patronage include representatives of various dynasties. Here, as in Japan, it was not so much a question of whether Buddhism was to be declared the state religion as such as whether other interested parties (such as Confucians, Daoists, or Shinto bureaucrats, for example) might persuade the ruler that these interlopers represented a threat to imperial power—not to mention to the influence of the indigenous religious establishment. One could list a number of other instances, but the point to keep in mind is that if an outsider religion is to prosper, it needs political patronage of some kind.

13. Were there any further stages of development in sacred literature, as happened in, for example, Hinduism or Judaism?

Like the sacred texts of both Hinduism and Judaism, those of Buddhism developed over many centuries and include an enormous range of themes and literary types. There the similarity ends, for two main reasons. First, unlike either the Hindu or Judaic scriptures, which were composed almost exclusively in a single carefully preserved canonical language (Sanskrit and Hebrew), Buddhism's scriptures were written in a number of different languages and translated liberally. Even before Buddhism ever left India, major texts existed in both Pali and Sanskrit. Second, there is not nearly the kind of unanimity as to the content of a Buddhist canon as one finds in either Hinduism or Judaism. The vast majority of Hindus acknowledge the authority of at least the Vedas and the Upanishads; most Jews that of at least the Torah strictly so-called. In Buddhist history, the elaboration of sacred texts has generally betokened division rather than unity.

Buddhist scriptural development outside of India took two principal forms: translation of Sanskrit texts and other documents of Indian origin, and composition of new texts in regional languages. The result is a massive library that is very likely the world's largest collection of canonical religious texts. Not all Buddhists claim the collection as authoritative or even acknowledge the existence of the full complement.

In fact, the general pattern of development is that individual groups became organized around the teaching of one or a few texts, proclaiming them as the sole authoritative scriptures. Aside from the Indian Pali Canon, however, there are two other major canonical collections. The Chinese canon, called the "Great Scripture-Store," includes more than a thousand separate texts, including many commentaries originally written in Chinese, and was first compiled in the late tenth century. An even more massive Tibetan canon contains two major sections, the Kanjur (Translation of the Words of Buddha) and Tanjur (Translation of Teachings of Buddha), in some 320 volumes, much apparently translated from Sanskrit originals now lost.

14.   How did Buddhism take root and grow in China?

Buddhism's transformation into a Chinese tradition began during the age of the powerful Han dynasty (206 B.C.E.–220 C.E.). According to legend, the Han emperor Ming Ti had a dream around the year 61 that prompted him to send emissaries to India for Buddhist teachers, texts, and art. Travelers from India could choose several land routes, including one over the Himalayas and one to the northeast through Burma, but Buddhist missionaries generally preferred a route through Central Asia. Setting out from northwest India, the early missionary monks made their way through Afghanistan into Central Asia, areas in which Buddhism had found a welcome during Ashoka's reign, and then on to Kashgar on the old silk road. Skirting a high desert to either the north or south, the monks headed east to the sacred Buddhist caves of Dun Huang on the northwest border of Han China. From there they would direct their steps to any of several imperial cities.

During the Han dynasty, an important Buddhist community grew at the capital of Lo-yang, on the Yellow River in northeast China. It is likely that the Lo-yang community had begun some years before the Emperor Ming Ti came to power and that the story of his dream developed as a way of legitimating Buddhism's presence by association with imperial patronage. In any case, the young Chinese Buddhist community had gained sufficient strength by around 150 that a sizable new contingent of missionary translators from India could undertake a serious proselytizing campaign. By the end of the Han period, the monastic *sangha* was becoming firmly established, accepting Chinese aspirants, and beginning to send out its own monks on mission and in search of sacred texts to translate.

For the next 500 years, Buddhism flourished with the help of the imperial patronage of several dynasties. By around 350, it had become the single largest religious tradition in China, and by 450 the faith had both survived its first experience of persecution and was accepted by the majority of the population. A milestone and measure of Buddhism's inculturation was the appearance of the first works of Chinese Buddhist art during the fifth century. That same period witnessed the growth of several distinct sects or denominations of Buddhism, each representing an adaptation to different religious emphases in Confucianism and Daoism. From the beginning, Buddhism's fortunes in China were intimately bound up with its ability to demonstrate the compatibility of its teachings with the two indigenous Chinese traditions. But in the year 845, fortune turned against Buddhism when a Daoist emperor of the T'ang dynasty decided to purge his realm of the foreign influence. Hardest hit in the persecution were the smaller sects that lacked material resources, while the sects known as Pure Land *(Ching-t'u-tsung)* and Ch'an survived. Over the next several centuries, a revival of neo-Confucianism continued to put pressure on the Pure Land Buddhists, leaving only Ch'an, the forerunner of that most widely known branch of Buddhism, Zen, with room to grow.

15. Which principal varieties of Buddhism developed in China?

Of the eight major varieties of Chinese Buddhism that had blossomed by the seventh century, Pure Land and Ch'an were the largest and most influential. Though some of Pure Land's central practices and teachings appeared as early as the Han dynasty, tradition counts Hui Yuan (344–416) and T'an Luan (476–543) among the earliest teachers, the one laying the foundations and the other further developing its focus on Amitabha Buddha. Emphasis on various devotional practices that were not difficult to learn (such as visualization of the Buddha, vocal formulae designed to confer immortality, and brief focusing of one's thoughts in a form of simple meditation) made Pure Land widely attractive. Amitabha, the Buddha of Infinite Light, presided over the Western Paradise, the "pure land" to which all faithful devotees hoped to be delivered. A central teaching is that complete trust in the Buddha's saving grace and power yields a form of enlightenment suited to the average lay person. At the heart of this enlightenment is faith, which is given expression in continual calling on the saving power with the words "Glory to Amitabha Buddha." As a matter of emphasis, Pure Land represents an appeal to a saving power, with good works considered secondary to faith. Pure Land came to be known as the "easy path" to enlightenment, slow, low key, but certain to yield results. Between the believer and the saving Buddha called Amitabha stands the mediating bodhisattva Kwan Yin ("One who hears sounds [i.e., prayers]"), ever accessible and ready to bestow grace on all who ask. By about 650, Pure Land was the dominant devotional trend in China and would eventually become very important in Japan as well.

At least two important Indian schools of Buddhist scholasticism, heavily philosophical in tone and content, took root early on in China. They were the Hua-yen or "Flower Garland" school, based on the Avatamsaka Sutra, and the T'ien-t'ai or "Celestial Platform" school, whose central scripture was the Lotus Sutra. Some Chinese Buddhist teachers reacted against their dry logic and formalistic approach to arcane questions, arguing that these schools were mired down in their own verbiage and were losing sight of the goal of enlightenment. One of those critics was Bodhidharma (d. 532), Ch'an's first patriarch and a teacher who emphasized the discipline of "deep meditation," *dhyana* in Sanskrit, *ch'an* in Chinese, *zen* in Japanese. Bodhidharma's intense concentration became the kernel around which many fantastic legends grew. Popular iconography still depicts the patriarch as virtually all eyes that are loosely connected to an evanescent body that has all but evaporated. He and subsequent patriarchs stressed spiritual insight gained by direct transmission from teacher to disciple, bypassing all spurious scriptural texts and doctrinal treatises.

Experience alone counts, with meditation a tool toward a flash of realization, a once-and-for-all jolt of enlightenment very different from what the poet Gerard Manley Hopkins might have called the "lingering-out sweet skill" of Pure Land devotionalism. Ch'an teachers did not always agree, however, on the desired results of their practice of meditation; some, especially in the south of China, took exception with the northern emphasis on relatively long, slow meditative discipline, arguing that it was too gradual. Several distinct schools had developed by the mid-ninth century, and two have remained significant. The "Five Ranks" (Ts'ao-tung) lineage, founded by I-hsuan (d. 867), taught the use of a

GEOGRAPHICAL SPREAD OF BUDDHISM

Mahayana = ++++++++++++++++

Theravada = —————

Vajrayana = =>>>>>>>>>>

	600 B.C.E.	250 B.C.E.	100 C.E.	450 C.E.	800 C.E.	1150 C.E.	1500 C.E.	1850 C.E.	2000 C.E.
India	++++++++++++++++++++++++++++++++++ >>>>>>>>>>>>>>>>>> >>>>> ++++++++								
Tibet	=========================>>>>>>>>>>>>>>>>>>>								
Sri Lanka	———————————————————————								
SE Asia	++++ ————————————————————————								
China	++								
Korea	+++++++++++++++++++++++++++++++++++++++								
Japan	++++++++++++++++++++++++++++++++++								

meditative regimen over many years; but the "Shouting and Striking" (Lin-chi) school, founded by Liang-chieh (807–869), sought more immediate results through the use of arresting methods designed to shock the aspirant out of dependence on linear thinking. Both schools take a "subitist" (or sudden-enlightenment) approach, by contrast with the more gradual method of Pure Land. Even a practitioner of the drawn-out discipline of the Five Ranks school might receive enlighten-ment in one dramatic moment, as though struck by lightning.

16. What were the circumstances of Buddhism's origins and growth in Japan?

Buddhism came to Japan by way of Korea much the way it had come to China and Korea, with missionary monks and enough royal support to allow it to take root. Late in the fourth century, a Chinese monk had introduced Buddhism to the city that became present-day Pyongyang, the capital of North Korea. By the sixth century, Buddhism enjoyed the royal favor of both the Koguryo dynasty in the north and the Paekche dynasty further south. Around 552 the Paekche king sent a Buddha image and several Buddhist sacred scriptures as a gift to the Japanese emperor Kimmei. Powerful families of the Japanese nobility squabbled as to whether to welcome a foreign cult to the islands, but Buddhism found the door opened by the victorious Soga clan. In a royal Constitution (602), Emperor Shotoku (574–622) decreed Buddhism's official acceptance in the land of the Kami, the deities of the indigenous tradition called Shinto. Shotoku built the temple complex of Horyu-ji outside of Nara and sent monks back to Korea and China to gather more scriptural texts and Buddhist art.

During the next two centuries, Chinese and Korean monks brought to Japan a succession of six different Buddhist lineages of Chinese ori-gin. Each of these lineages had originally developed around separate Indian Sanskrit scriptural texts. Four lineages were introduced into Japan during the seventh century, the Sanron, Jojitsu (a Hinayana school), Kusha, and Hosso schools. But only the Hosso gained anything like wide popularity; the others may have failed to catch on because of the abstract, speculative nature of their scriptural teachings. Two eighth century imports to the capital at Nara, the Ritsu (Hinayana) and Kegon lineages, presented a somewhat less esoteric interpretation of Buddhism. Along with the Hosso school, the Kegon still operates on a relatively small scale from headquarters in Nara.

During the ninth century, after the imperial capital had been moved to Kyoto, two new and very influential lineages arrived in Japan. In 805 a monk named Saicho (also called Dengyo Daishi, 767–822) founded a school called Tendai based on the Lotus of the Good Law sutra. His lineage, a transplant of the Chinese T'ien-t'ai school, sought to promote reconciliation between Buddhism and Shinto. Saicho established his center on Mount Hiei, near Kyoto, and began to ordain monks according to Mahayana precepts there. Just a year later, a monk named Kukai (also called Kobo Daishi, 744–835) brought his version of the Chinese Chen-yen (or True Word) lineage, known in Japan as the Shingon sect. Kukai made Mount Koya home to his school, thus inaugurating a sort of battle of the holy mountains.

Both Tendai and Shingon initially sought to offer a style of Buddhism more broadly appealing than the earlier lineages. But as Tendai grew more speculative and Shingon more mystical and esoteric, they tended to attract relatively small followings among the wealthy and well educated. However, Tendai's influence would spread through the reforming activities of several of its most famous monks, and Shingon remains a significant presence in contemporary Japanese Buddhism.

Teachings of Pure Land Buddhism came to Japan when the Tendai monk Ennin (793–864) returned from his studies in China, introducing the practice of invoking Amida's name. Several other monks developed the teachings over the next century and a half, but Japan did not witness the widespread growth of truly "popular" forms of Buddhism until the twelfth century. Three new lineages branched off from the Tendai school during the twelfth and thirteenth centuries. A monk of Mount Hiei named Honen (1133–1212) formally established the Pure Land school in Japan, emphasizing the perfect efficacy of a ritual invocation of Amida, the Buddha of the Western Paradise. Two other Tendai monks (Eisai and Dogen) founded the main branches of Japanese Zen, and a monk named Nichiren (1222–1282) began a sect based on the mere repetition of the *name* of the Lotus of the Good Law sutra, around which Tendai had originally formed.

17. What are the most important schools of Japanese Buddhism?

Pure Land, or Jodoshu, and a "reformed" version called True Pure Land (Jodo Shinshu) together form arguably the largest single group of Japanese Buddhists. Tendai monk Honen (1133–1212) found his studies on Mount Hiei too narrow and decided to develop an interpretation that would address the needs of a wider public. He advocated a ritual called *nembutsu,* calling on the name of the Buddha, which consisted of protracted repetition of the phrase *Namu Amida Butsu* ("Glory to Amida Buddha"). Honen's teaching quickly became so popular that powers in competing schools saw to it that he was exiled in 1207. Not long after he returned, Honen's principal disciple, Shinran (1173–1262), parted company with his teacher. Shinran wanted a still more popular approach with which the masses of lay Buddhists could identify. He left the monastic life to marry and continued to preach devotion to Amida as well as to the *bodhisattva* Kannon (Japanese form of the Chinese Kwan Yin) and the "Buddha of the Future" known as Miroku (Maitreya in Sanskrit). Between them, these two lineages currently have more than 30,000 temples in Japan.

Japan's two major Zen lineages together comprise a second large segment of the country's population. When Eisai (1141–1215) traveled from Mount Hiei to China he discovered that Tendai's Chinese forebear was losing ground, while the Ch'an schools were spreading. Eisai gathered texts central to the Lin-chi Ch'an school and returned home to establish its Japanese equivalent, Rinzai Zen. Emphasizing what Pure Land critics called "self-power" rather than the "other-power" advocated by more popular forms of Buddhist teaching, Rinzai uses decidedly confrontational methods to help aspirants break old mental and spiritual habits. Eisai believed in supplementing *zazen,* or meditational sitting, with judicious physical and mental disciplines. Tendai monk Dogen (1200–1253), one of Japanese Buddhism's most famous figures, also traveled to China and studied the Ts'ao-tung, or Five Ranks, lineage of Ch'an. He opted for a quieter, less psychically disruptive approach that emphasized silent enlightenment through meditation.

Nichiren's lineage, fifth-largest of Japan's Buddhist groups, may be the school best known outside of Japan apart from Zen. In recent years a number of U.S. celebrities, such as popular singer Tina Turner, have gone public with their belief in the salutary effects of chanting the Japanese mantra, *"Namu Myoho-renge-kyo"* ("Praise to the Lotus of the

Good Law Sutra"). More than a few modern-day groups trace their origins to Nichiren.

Shingon remains perhaps the third- or fourth-largest single segment of Japanese Buddhism, counting more than 12,000 temples, twice that number of teachers, and some 12 million adherents as of 1962. An important clue to the esoteric bent of the school is that the name *shin-gon* is the Japanese pronunciation of the Chinese translation of the Sanskrit word *mantra,* a particularly potent word or phrase given to an individual devotee. Reasons some scholars list for its thriving into modern times include its flexibility in incorporating non-Buddhist concepts, and its being the only esoteric lineage of its kind around for hundreds of years. I would add to that *shingon's* tradition of striking iconography, reminiscent in some ways of Tibetan Buddhism's extraordinary visual repertoire.

18. Could you say more about the two branches of Zen?

Eisai's Rinzai lineage, now roughly one-third the size of Dogen's Soto school, employs a number of distinctive and intriguing methods. Monks gather for *zazen* in a large rectangular room with platforms, perhaps a foot and a half high, running along lengthwise on two sides. During meditation sessions, a senior monk equipped with a wooden switch paces slowly up and down the room watching for signs of drowsiness or distraction in the meditators. If he detects such a sign, or if a meditator communicates by a small gesture that he wants assistance, the switch master stands before the individual who then bends forward slightly to receive a pair of stinging blows to the upper back. The idea is not to do harm but to bring about a return of concentration. Shouting is the audible equivalent of striking and is meant to help the meditator regain focus.

The mental counterpart to this physical discipline is the koan, sometimes called the "Zen riddle," which the Zen master *(roshi)* assigns the meditator during a brief session of "spiritual direction." "What is the sound of one hand clapping?" is perhaps the best known example of a koan. Its purpose is to derail the meditator's accustomed ways of thinking, demonstrating the bankruptcy of reliance on reason. Enlightenment is not something one can "figure out" as one might solve some practical problem. One arrives at the goal only by letting go of all preconceived intellectual agendas, and the koan is meant to help the meditator get beyond the anxiety created by a problem that seems to have no solution. As an arrow sails toward its target by being released, not by being hurled, so the seeker moves toward enlightenment only by letting go of the energy accumulated as he or she experiences increasingly the futility of logic.

Soto Zen uses less confrontational techniques, relying mainly on protracted meditation in which regular breathing helps establish bodily equilibrium. Strictly speaking, *zazen* is not a means to enlightenment, but the very act of attaining the goal, which is the realization that the Buddha-nature already exists within the individual. To be more precise, all beings *are* the Buddha-nature. The Buddha-nature is simultaneously the possibility and the actuality of enlightenment, and it exists in all things as water exists in ice or forest in tree. Because all of reality is condensed into each moment, attentiveness to the "now" is the way to enlightenment. As each "now" is fleeting, so even the Buddha-nature shares the quality of impermanence inherent in all things. To the question, "Doesn't that mean that the seeker is chasing a mirage?" Dogen might respond, "You do have a problem, don't you? Be who and where you are. The reality you seek is not someone or somewhere else. Cease striving to become, for what you seek to be, you are." In meditation the meditator becomes aware of and sets aside all thoughts as they arise; then becomes aware of both thinking and nonthinking without fixating on either; and finally arrives at the peacefulness of simple consciousness.

Dogen brought back to Japan his understanding of the Chinese "Five Ranks" school of Ch'an, so-called because of its teaching of five steps toward realization of the identity of the absolute and the relative. Through meditation, one first focuses on the existence of the Buddha-nature within the self and then sees the self within the Buddha-nature. In steps three and four, the seeker focuses in turn on the Buddha-nature as though it existed alone, and on the self and the world of appearances to realize that they enjoy no independent existence and are therefore empty. Finally, awareness of the emptiness of all things yields to the realization that the absolute and the relative are purely and simply one. Eternal and transient, necessary and contingent, substantial and apparent, simple Buddha-nature and the "ten thousand things" of the phenomenal world, full void and empty fullness—all come together in the final goal of meditation that is called *satori*. Soto Zen is, after True Pure Land, the second largest Buddhist sect in Japan today.

19. Is the Buddhism of Southeast Asia similar to that of China, Korea, and Japan?

Buddhism traveled to most of the Southeast Asian nations from India and Sri Lanka. As a result, the Theravada lineage predominates there. Buddha's teaching came to Burma as early as Ashoka's time, but the tradition was fairly well established in China by the time it first began to make its way beyond Burma to Thailand and the rest of Southeast Asia. For several centuries, Burmese Buddhism was a mixture of varieties, but the patronage of a late eleventh-century monarch who had been converted by a monk from Sri Lanka gradually turned his people toward Theravada. Burma has been a haven of Theravada scholarship ever since. South and east of Burma lay the Indochinese peninsula, now occupied by Thailand, Laos, Cambodia, and Vietnam. Parts of the peninsula were for a time ruled by Hindu kings, but Mahayana Buddhism began to make inroads as early as the mid-sixth century. Beginning in the thirteenth century, Theravada influence began to grow in Cambodia and eventually supplanted both Mahayana Buddhism and the remnants of Hinduism over most of the region.

Vietnam is a special case in that, though India was the earliest source of its Buddhist traditions, later missionaries from China introduced Mahayana lineages that took firm hold, and Chinese influence was broader there than in neighboring lands. Notions of divine kingship won the favor of several rulers in the ninth and tenth centuries, so the Buddhism of royal patronage remained tinged with Hinduism. But from about 1000 to 1400, Chinese Mahayana lineages including Pure Land and Ch'an flourished. Increasing influence of Confucian officialdom made life difficult for Buddhists through the early modern period; then Buddhism enjoyed a renewal prior to the fall of Saigon in 1975.

20. Could you describe the kinds of Buddhism predominant in the Himalayan nations, such as Nepal, Tibet, and Bhutan?

The land of Buddha's birth, Nepal knew Buddhism from the start, but today the kingdom remains predominantly Hindu, harboring only small enclaves of Buddhists. Nepal's neighbors on the "roof of the world" in Tibet went almost entirely for Buddhism, however, and have been for centuries home of an intriguing branch of the tradition called Vajrayana, the "Thunderbolt Vehicle." Tibetan, and Himalaya Buddhism generally, is known as Vajrayana because of the ritual use of the *vajra,* a symbol of imperishable diamond, of thunder and lightning. Some scholars identify Tibetan Buddhism as one of four branches of a group of sects called Tantrayana; others classify it as an example of the original form of Mahayana. One thing seems clear: Remote as Tibet may be, it came under the influence of religious sources from virtually all around it, including various forms of Buddhism.

At the center of Tibetan Buddhism is the religious figure called the *lama,* Tibetan for "guru," source of yet another of its names, *Lamaism.* Several major lineages of lamas developed, beginning in the ninth century with the Nyingma-pa. Two centuries later, the Sarma-pa divided into the Sakya-pa and Kagyu-pa. Three hundred years later, one of Tibet's most revered lamas, Tsong-kha-pa (1357–1419), founded the reforming Gelug-pa. Followers acclaimed the lineage's third teacher as an incarnation of the bodhisattva Avalokiteshvara (known in China as Kwan Yin and in Japan as Kannon), thus inaugurating the line of Dalai Lamas, the fourteenth and most recent of whom was born in 1935. Important aspects of Tibetan thought center on the conviction that the bodhisattva, a Buddha who has foregone final nirvana in order to remain available out of compassion for all sentient beings, is continually among us.

Lamaist life revolves around the monastery to an even greater degree than Buddhist life of most other varieties. During the centuries, vast numbers of men and women have become monks and nuns, some reports claiming fully 20 percent of the population. Like the monastic traditions of other religions, that of Tibet has had its high and low points, but through Tibetan history the monastery has been the guardian of culture and education. Among Tibetan monasticism's enduring achievements is the luxuriant religious iconography of the colorful mandala designs that meditators use to visualize and enter into altered psychic states identified as temporary forms of deification. These highly esoteric rituals are available only to advanced lamas, while the majority of the populace practice a syncretistic mix of shamanism, ancient Tibetan spiritualism, and other imported religious practices.

21. Has Buddhism become especially associated with particular cities the way that Hinduism has with Banaras or that Islam has with Mecca?

In lands deeply influenced by Buddhist tradition, no single city exercises quite the religious magnetism of either Banaras or Mecca. However, certain cities in virtually every region we now identify as nation-states have taken on a sort of national status among Buddhists, and in one or two instances a much broader prestige has kept Buddhist pilgrims coming from considerable distances. Sites associated with key events in Buddha's life, such as Bodhgaya, Lumbini Grove (where he was born), and Sarnath have been important pilgrim goals off and on through history, depending on political circumstances and ease of travel. But most holy places have been hallowed by more remote associations, by the presence of relics, or by affiliation with some much later holy person.

Anuradhapura, sometimes called the Rome of the Theravadins, is Sri Lanka's ancient capital and best-known Buddhist city, home to noted religious scholars and several important major stupas. Mandalay in Burma projects a similar aura, as does Rangoon, both bursting with famous gold-leaf-covered temples and the sites, respectively, of the fifth (1856–1857) and sixth (1954–1956) Buddhist councils, which were convened to verify the accuracy of the Tripitaka. Rangoon and Mandalay eclipsed the medieval capital of Pagan after the latter was abandoned in the wake of Mongol invasions in 1287. Overlooked by the massive Potala palace-monastery, the Tibetan city of Lhasa was the spiritual center of Vajrayana Buddhism prior to the brutal Chinese crackdown on Tibet in 1959, but that changed with the exile of the Dalai Lama and the destruction of hundreds of monasteries and temples.

Cities important to Mahayana Buddhists are more numerous because of the wider dispersion of Mahayana lineages. In Japan, Nara and Kyoto, the country's first and second capital cities, are at the top of the list. Kyoto boasts some 1,500 Buddhist temples and monasteries; Koya and Hiei, two mountains most sacred to Japanese Buddhists, are not far away. Korea's Kyongju ranks as a sort of cathedral city, with the ancient Pulguksa and several other important temples, and as the long-ago capital of Korea for 1,000 years. Legend says that the first king of the Silla dynasty to accept Buddhism built Pulguksa in 535. China, the first and largest of the Mahayana Buddhist missionary conquests, also embraces the largest number of important sites. Some of those have been cities but generally not for specifically religious reasons. During the almost 19 centuries of Buddhist presence in China prior to the Maoist revolution, the most important cities were not surprisingly the capitals of the various emperors who chose to favor the tradition and thus protect it from persecution.

THREE:

DOCTRINES AND PRACTICES

22. What is the function of doctrine in the Buddhist scheme of things?

Buddha once engaged a man named Malunkyaputta in a discussion of the seductive nature of speculation and the futility of addiction to theoretical questions. According to a "sermon" account in the second section of the Pali Canon's Sutra Pitaka, Malunkyaputta had threatened to leave the sangha unless the Buddha gave definitive answers to his queries about the nature of the world, body, soul, life after death, and a host of other issues. You, replied the Buddha, are like a person who had been shot with a poisoned arrow who fends off the ministrations of his friends, insisting that he needs more information before he will allow them to remove the shaft. Until he determines his assailant's name, caste, place of origin, and physical characteristics, of what material the weapons were made, and what bird's feathers guided the arrow to its mark, he will not allow the surgeon to do his work. Such a one will die before attaining his intellectual goal.

Stick to the fundamental issues of ordinary experience, the Buddha counseled. People like Malunkyaputta impose needless burdens on themselves and others. *Dharma* is like a raft *(yana)* in that its purpose is to convey one from the shores of ignorance to the shores of enlightenment. When you've reached the other shore, it makes no sense to strap the raft to your back and lug it around forever. Discard it on the shore and move on. Scripture notes Malunkyaputta's enormous feeling of relief at the good news. Nevertheless, Buddhism's various schools have elaborated their doctrines, often in minutest detail, but generally with the caveat that it was all just so much vain talk by way of concession to the conventions of ordinary language.

Numerous other metaphors for dharma are helpful in understanding the role of doctrine. Because the Teaching functions as the ongoing presence of the Buddha on earth, it is analogous to the Holy Spirit for Christians, except that dharma is not personified. Like the Buddha and the lotus, dharma is "mud-born," unsullied though mired in the muck and dependent on it for life. Dharma is a wheel to be turned, and that takes effort. As one of the "three jewels," dharma is indestructible, like

41

the Buddha and the sangha. Most of all, Buddhists think of the dharma as a source of light and beauty; ultimately to be discarded, it is nevertheless healing in a world of suffering. One is well advised to appreciate it as such.

23. Is there a fundamental Buddhist creed?

Fine points of Buddhist belief vary enormously from place to place and sect to sect, but there is unanimous agreement on the centrality of the "Three Jewels." The most basic statement of faith for Buddhists is the threefold affirmation, "I take refuge in the Buddha. I take refuge in the dharma. I take refuge in the sangha." Each of these "jewels"— teacher, teaching, and community—radiates its own light, but they are all set in a single crown. It may seem paradoxical that a tradition that so insists on the temporary value of doctrine also insists that adherents begin by committing themselves to living in that triple light, but many religious traditions seem to begin by attempting to lay down principles that believers must ultimately transcend.

For Theravada Buddhists, taking refuge in the Buddha means adhering to the teaching of Shakyamuni, the Buddha of this aeon, bearing in mind that he enjoined his followers to be lamps unto their own feet, rather than expect another to save them. For Buddhists of the various Mahayana lineages, refuge in the Buddha means calling upon the cosmic saving power of the Enlightened One now both hidden and manifest, both infinitely removed from the world of suffering and immediately accessible through the gracious compassion of the bodhisattva.

Taking refuge in the dharma also has different implications, depending on the refuge taker's specific affiliation within the greater Buddhist fold. But in general it means committing oneself to learn and understand what the Buddha taught. Buddhists in India and Central Asia founded some of the world's earliest and greatest "universities," each dedicated to propagating the dharma and elaborating its various linguistic, legal, and philosophical sub-disciplines. Though such an education has typically been available only to monks, the average Buddhist lay person can take refuge in the dharma both by seeking instruction on a more limited basis and by taking his or her own ordinary experience of life as seriously as Siddhartha did his. Much more than intellectual content, however, dharma is also the promise of genuine contentment, rapturous light, unbounded loving kindness, the hope of profoundest peace for all things living.

Seeking community, the believer takes refuge in the assembly called the sangha. Laymen and -women belong to the sangha just as do monks and nuns, but the monastic organization eventually came to be identified generally as the *real* sangha, or at least that aspect of Buddhist community to which one can go for spiritual shelter. Theravada Buddhists have been especially attached to this narrower definition of sangha, but even in Mahayana lands the monastic option has often represented a higher calling. In many Buddhist communities, young men still enter monasteries for a few months, as a rite of passage. For some Mahayana Buddhists the sangha embraces all sentient beings without discrimination, for all are destined for salvation in due time. The three refuges thus have a range of meanings, but at least in their broadest significance they represent an important common link among the world's Buddhists.

24. What are the most basic elements in Buddhist teaching?

At the heart of *dharma* are the basic elements that formed the content of the Buddha's own experience of enlightenment, the Four Noble Truths. Articulated with elegant and disarming simplicity, the Noble Truths can slip by if one is expecting some arcane riddle, but then, even the traditional sage utterance is not all it's cracked up to be. I am reminded of an amusing radio commercial of years ago in which a seeker of truth struggles for weeks to climb a peak whereon the great teacher sits in meditation. Clambering over the summit, the spent pilgrim asks about the meaning of life. "Life is like a running brook," the guru tells him. "Life is like a running brook!? What's that supposed to mean?" the seeker retorts. Says the guru, "You mean life is *not* like a running brook?" The Buddha would not back down so easily. Yes, he might say, it really does come down to Four Noble Truths.

First, life is suffering. Many people immediately respond either by dismissing this as too obvious to bear repeating or too negative to be of any use—"And it took him how long to figure that out?" What the statement really means is not the least bit obvious to most of us who keep thinking that life is not supposed to be this way. On the other hand, the statement does not counsel grim teeth-gritting acceptance of one's sad lot. Face it and move on—to the second truth: Craving is the cause of

MAJOR DOCTRINAL THEMES

The Four Noble Truths

1. Life is suffering (*duhkha*).
2. Craving is the cause of suffering.
3. In order to end suffering, one must end craving.
4. The means to end craving is the Noble Eightfold Path:

The Noble Eightfold Path

Threefold Training

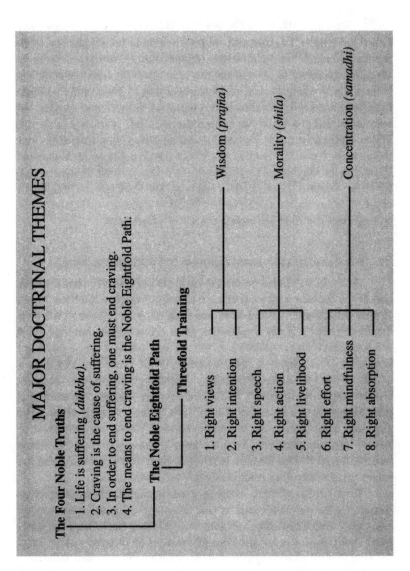

1. Right views
2. Right intention   Wisdom (*prajña*)

3. Right speech
4. Right action   Morality (*shila*)
5. Right livelihood

6. Right effort
7. Right mindfulness   Concentration (*samadhi*)
8. Right absorption

suffering. Behind this truth is a wealth of observation of the human scene. Craving or grasping here means all inappropriate, obsessive gotta-have-it (or, for that matter, I'll-do-anything-to-avoid-it) motivation. Buddhism is a "middle" way between hedonism and austerity, between pursuit and avoidance.

Third, to remove the cause of suffering, put an end to disordered craving. That presupposes that one understands the two other essential characteristics of existence that, along with suffering, constitute the human predicament, namely, impermanence and nonself, themes taken up in greater detail in the next question. In simple terms, the third truth affirms that it is possible to undo the suffering caused by desire for independence and individuality by coming to a clear appreciation of how impermanence definitively undermines all such desires. Finally, to break free of enthralling hopes and fears, follow the Eightfold Path. The path's main goals are wisdom, morality, and concentration (sometimes called the Threefold Training). Wisdom *(prajña)* comprises right views, knowledge of the Four Truths; and right intention, compassionate disposition toward all, neither stubborn nor apathetic. Morality *(shila)* includes the next three steps on the path, namely, right speech, refraining from all sins of the tongue; right action, refraining from killing, stealing, and inappropriate sexual behavior; and right livelihood, engaging only in nonharmful occupations (ruling out, for example, trading in weapons or slaves). Concentration *(samadhi)* requires right effort, just enough attention to one's occupation; right mindfulness, reflection on the deeper meaning of the Four Truths; and right absorption, a foretaste of nirvana in which one learns to seek happiness in neither anxiety nor overeagerness.

25. The formulation of the Four Noble Truths seems very schematic. Does Buddhist teaching analyze the human condition in greater detail?

Once upon a time, a group of children came to play at the banks of a river. All along the beach, the children began to construct castles in the sand. They were very possessive, each making sure that no one else made a claim on their castle. After they had finished building, one youngster kicked over another's castle and leveled it. Its builder became furious, began to beat the aggressor, and called to his friends to come and help him beat up the destroyer. They came running, ganging up on the child, kicking him and pummeling him with sticks. Returning to their castles, they warned all the others to keep their distance. "Mine," they all cried, "you can't have it!" As evening drew on, they all decided that it was time to go home. They no longer cared about their castles. One leveled his with his hands; another kicked his and stomped it flat. Then they all went back to their own homes.

So goes the "Parable of Me and Mine," in paraphrase. This little tale of futility sums up what early Buddhist formulations refer to as the three features of existence: suffering *(duhkha),* impermanence *(anitya),* and nonself *(anatman).* The first feature is at the core of the First Noble Truth, but the other two need further attention here. Someone once asked a famous psychiatrist what he thought were the marks of a genuinely mature person. A profound awareness of mortality and life's brevity, the willingness to engage life without holding back, and the ability to see the humor in the irony of it all, the doctor replied. I suspect the Buddha would concur.

Impermanence is the cause of suffering, from the Buddhist perspective, but the tradition has kept its analysis of impermanence more or less separate in the interest of maintaining its clear formulation of the Four Noble Truths. As Shakespeare observes that "Ruin hath taught me thus to ruminate," so virtually any reflective person will eventually conclude that nothing lasts forever and will resolve at some level to act accordingly. Ironically, the human capacity for denial of even the most obvious realities comes about as close to permanence as one can get. Most of us have inherited the cultural tendency to keep pressing the search for an "unmoved mover," an underlying stability whose permanence we hope will somehow rub off on lesser beings. Buddhist teaching recommends that we simply call off the search for what is only the product of wishful thinking and deal with the hard realities of experience. Even so, the Buddha might agree with Shakespeare's "love that well which thou must leave ere long." How to love well is the challenge.

No Buddhist teaching cuts as close to the bone, however, as the concept of nonself. Like suffering, nonself is a consequence of impermanence. All things are impermanent, including the various constituents of human personality; if even those come and go, one must conclude that the idea of a stable center or soul makes no sense. In Buddha's day, a "substantialist" Hindu psychology was anchored in an indestructible soul *(atman).* Buddha argued that the Hindu concern for liberating this soul was just one more unhelpful form of craving and a serious distraction from the most pressing project of all, attending to one's experience here and now. Lose the eschatological hopes and fears attached to concern for the soul, Buddha taught; therein lies radical freedom. But his process-oriented psychology is a bitter pill. Many people find the idea that there is no independent center, no essence of individuality, no soul holding the human person together very unsettling. Most of us simply assume, and indeed depend on, the existence of a substantial ego without which personhood makes no sense. That, of course, is precisely what the Buddha was getting at: Assume nothing, depend on nothing that is bound up in the fundamental reality of impermanence. The greater one's terror at the thought that there is no immortal soul, the clearer the need to let go of an idea that turns out to be the most insidious of all causes of suffering.

26. The characteristics of impermanence and suffering seem fairly clear, but the idea of the *nonself* is very puzzling. Could you say more about it?

Hinduism teaches that "salvation" entails liberation from endless cycles of rebirth in which the indestructible soul transmigrates to a new embodied existence. Buddhists also talk about rebirth but because there is no individual "soul," one has to ask what or who is reborn. Numerous other questions arise in the face of this arresting notion of no-soul. Buddhist tradition has sought to answer them with closely reasoned argument. If at times the answers appear only to raise new questions, it helps to recall that the Buddhist rejection of Hinduism's soul theory was primarily a way of focusing the attention of each person on immediate experience, not an attempt to construct a theory as such. In other words, the concept of no-soul is a linchpin in the Buddha's teaching that one has to begin with the bare human condition independent of metaphysical speculation. Compared to Buddha's scalpel, Ockham's razor is a rusty butter knife. Positing an independent, incorruptible soul, the Buddha argued, only aggravates the human tendency to alienation from self.

If there is no soul to hold together this thing called a person, then what is it that produces the experience of personhood, of individuality? Buddhist psychology defines *personality* as a collection of five aggregates or "heaps" *(skandhas)*. These are clusters of experiences that constitute

physical form, sensation, perception, mental formations, and consciousness, all bonded together by craving. The greater the craving that holds
these shifting phenomena together, the more intense the suffering at every
level of experience, from the most physical to the most intangible. Gradual diminution of disordered desire by means of meditative discipline
weakens the bond among the five aggregates until at last one is on the
verge of nirvana, the total cessation of ego formation. Then at death, nothing remains to be reembodied, and the "individual" achieves freedom
from all suffering.

But isn't freedom from suffering a kind of experience? If so, what
or who experiences it? Also, what happens if a person dies still firmly in
the grip of illusion, still seduced by the vain hope of permanence and
stubbornly defending "me and mine"? What, or who, then goes on to be
reborn if there's no soul? Here Buddhist teaching introduces the concept
of *chitta,* a form of transpersonal awareness, a form of pure energy that
embraces the entire mental and emotional spectrum. In the liberated person, it is the chitta that realizes freedom. In the person who dies short of
the goal, it is the chitta, representing an ongoing conviction of individuality, a fixation on the need for ego survival, that effects that very survival in another birth. Be careful what you wish for, because you *will* get
it! Critics argue that the Buddhist chitta is merely atman by another
name because a form of energy that survives death must be governed by
some fixed law. Buddhists counter that the enduring spiritual qualities of
knowledge, wisdom, benevolence, and compassion are the vehicle of
chitta, which is as protean as the five aggregates and not a stable sub-
stance like atman.

Buddhist analysis of no-soul is quite complicated, and, in general
people go on using conventional language of selfhood, but the basic purpose of the idea is not so hard to state: Complete freedom means holding
on to nothing. Period.

27. If you had to choose a single concept that you would call quintessentially Buddhist, one that would put all the others in the widest possible perspective, what would it be?

"Emptiness" *(shunyata)* does for Buddhists what "cosmic order
and individual destiny" *(dharma)* does for Hindus. You might even say
that, from a Buddhist perspective, "nothing" holds it all together. The

suggestion that "all things are empty" is not the sort of thing most Americans will find appealing, partly because it sounds entirely negative and partly because it seems to imply a denunciation of life in such a commodity-oriented society as ours. What fools must we be who chase endlessly after things to own to make ourselves feel better, a Buddhist might say. But the concept of emptiness is neither negative nor necessarily a condemnation intended to elicit feelings of guilt. Shunyata is rather a way of characterizing a whole state of being whose more obvious features are suffering and impermanence. We beat each other up for things no one will care about tomorrow. But what if one could adopt a truly useful attitude, one that could actually help one make sense of life?

Many of us find ourselves surrounded by the attitude that everything—and even everyone—is a means to get to something else. As a result, life becomes an endless series of negotiations, manipulations, and ulterior motives on a road that leads we know not where. Our hopes and fears prompt us to invest things and persons alike with a temporary but overwhelming importance determined by their value as stepping stones or rungs on a ladder. The Buddhist idea of *shunyata* means emptying all things of that kind of selfishly instrumental meaning, allowing them to mean only what they are in themselves, and appreciating them as such. That is the first step: every thing that is deserves my attention simply because it is, not for what it can do for me. "Suchness" is the other side of the coin of emptiness; it is the idea that I do not truly know anything until I know it purely as it is, for itself. So it turns out that the concept of emptiness is really a way to see things as full in a new way.

Step two is still more challenging, namely, the realization that nothing that exists does so in and of itself, but is part of a cosmic process of becoming and dying. As it turns out, all things are empty not only of the instrumental significance that we so readily see in them, but of independent existence as well. Everything is utterly dependent on everything else. Buddhist teaching describes this state of things with the "wheel of conditioned arising" (or dependent origination, *pratitya samutpada*). It reduces all existence to a circle of 12 interrelated causes, a cycle from which the meditator seeks release. Ignorance of the Four Truths (1) leads to action-impulses (2) which condition consciousness (3) in one being reborn, giving rise to mental and physical awareness (4) in the gathering of the five *skandhas,* leading to readiness of senses and mind (5) that disposes one to contact with one's environment (6) from which arise discrete sensations and perceptions (7). Craving (8) is followed by grasping (9) for a new birth, which leads to a new becoming (10), birth (11), and finally growth, death, decay (12), all resulting from ignorance, and the whole complex of suffering begins again.

In a way, then, all things really are empty in that they can neither come into being on their own nor secure their own survival however hard they try. Things and persons are impermanent because they have no substantial, indestructible core; it is the mistaken notion that they do possess such a core that causes all sentient beings to suffer—looking for something, not finding it, and yet insisting that it is there to be found rather than facing the facts of experience. "Emptiness" thus turns out to be a reminder of the need for proper perspective. Only the realization of the emptiness of all things brings genuine freedom because it liberates one from the tyranny of false expectations.

28. The term *nirvana* has made its way into popular jargon apparently as a kind of synonym for "zoned out"; how does Buddhism define the term?

Nir-vana literally means "no wind, no breath" and originally referred to a state in which an individual had completely extinguished the fires of craving. When one achieves such a state this side of death, Buddhist sources call it "nirvana with remainder." As a synonym for the Hindu term *moksha,* nirvana is often understood as release from *samsara,* the endless round of rebirth, a release possible completely only at death and involving the termination of individuality. When nirvana thus includes the end of anything like a personal entity that can survive death, it is called nirvana without remainder. It is closely linked to the concept of *nonself,* and its implications for Buddhist psychology in general are enormous.

Buddhist sources list a number of characteristics of nirvana that range from essential to more or less incidental. They describe the phenomenon as a pleasant experience of peacefulness, or "bliss," and liberation attainable in this life, involving increased knowledge, transformed consciousness, an absence of desire, and a sense of emptiness (in the best sense of that term!). The experience is said to presuppose a high level of ethical maturity and intense effort. An individual who experiences this state remains conscious but may have a dramatically diminished sense of separateness or individuality. Nirvana is likened to a meditative state in which the experiencer gains supernatural awareness and immeasurable well-being.

Virtually every Buddhist school has some distinctive view of nirvana. Mahayana lineages, for example, tend not to regard it as a separate order of being discrete from the experience of samsara. All schools seem to agree that a prime feature is utter clarity about the human condition. Transcending all dualities such as body and spirit, self and other, one who experiences nirvana enters a simple unity in which ordinary conflicts are resolved. How an individual who experiences nirvana this side of death could maintain the state uninterruptedly is indeed difficult to imagine, but one of the state's features is its permanence. By definition, therefore, one who appears to have attained nirvana and backslides has not attained it.

29. What do Buddhists think of death? Is there any notion of an afterlife?

When Buddhists meditate on death, it is not because they are particularly attracted to it but because it is a prime example of impermanence and because Buddha's first experience of death was among the Four Passing Sights. Most Buddhists grieve their losses and fear their own demises pretty much like the rest of us, but they see death from a very different perspective than Christians or Muslims, for example. There are, of course, those rare individuals for whom death is a definitive liberation from suffering, but popular belief in many Buddhist lands is that most people are destined for a stay in either heaven or hell, afterworlds that are not final destinations but part of the eternal flow of cycles. One's karma-balance at death determines whether one will spend a time in heaven or hell between births. A turn in hell is purgative, cleansing away bad karma from the most recent life.

Like some other traditional cosmologies, that of Mahayana Buddhism includes multiple heavens and hells representing varying degrees of pleasure or punishment. The Buddhist trilevel cosmos comprises the realm of sensual pleasure *(kamaloka),* the realm of form *(rupaloka),* and the realm of nonform *(arupaloka).* Perhaps the most famous of the heavens in the lowest realm is the Tushita heaven from which the Buddha of this aeon descended to Earth. The 13 to 18 heavens in the realm of form are the dwelling of purified gods. Those of the realm of no-form only the most spiritually advanced may enter. Mahayana tradition teaches that Buddhas and bodhisattvas have the power to save and bring devotees directly to the heavens over which they preside. Some lineages teach that salvation is all but assured to everyone who has the merest shred of faith.

Death and bereavement rituals vary from place to place, depending on local customs. In Thailand and Burma, families can hold funeral rites either in a temple or at home. When death is imminent the family begins preparations, gathering the various ritual items, candles, flowers, a bowl for cleansing the body, an image of the Buddha for the head of the bed, a book stand for the scriptures, and a small triple white flag symbolizing the Three Refuges. Principal Buddhist elements include chanting of texts from the Abhidharma Pitaka by local monks, a sermon on impermanence and life's ultimate purpose, nirvana. Cremation either at a cremation ground or in a temple follows at varying intervals, from several days to as much as a year for the most revered monks. Many Buddhists believe that attending to the final needs of the deceased is a way of securing merit for the dead person's next stage. For that purpose, those attending the cremation often declare their forgiveness for the deceased and ask for the same in return. Ashes are frequently interred in a funerary repository in a temple.

30.   Christian theologians talk of a Jesus of history and a Christ of faith; is there any parallel in Buddhist thought? If Mahayana Buddhism holds that the Buddha was more than a historical figure, did it evolve a way to describe his ongoing spiritual significance?

One could argue for a general Buddhist sense that the Enlightened One is both the Shakyamuni of history and the Buddha of faith. There are some interesting analogies but some very important differences as well. Theravada tradition certainly focuses on the historical teacher. On the other hand, there is nothing in Buddhism quite like the Christian understanding of the historical Jesus because Buddha was one of countless examples of an enlightened being in the world. But what about the Christian notion of the pre-existent *logos,* the idea that Christ existed eternally? This is still very different from the Buddhist concept of the *timelessness of the enlightened being* because of significant variations in the two traditions' understandings of history and time. The *bodhisattva* who eventually appears as the Buddha of the present aeon, Shakyamuni, enters the world over and over again but not as the same Buddha. Christian tradition holds that Jesus the Christ entered the world once and for all at the fullness of time and now reigns as Lord of a history that moves inexorably toward a conclusion at the end of time. In the Buddhist view, there will be no such end.

Both the Christian and Buddhist traditions nevertheless had to deal with the question of how and to what extent their central figures remained present and accessible to ordinary people after their departures from this Earth. Here is the question: How does an absolute transcendent reality also manifest itself immanently in the phenomenal world? Christian theologians expanded on scriptural allusions to a "cosmic" Christ and a Triune deity. Mahayana Buddhist thinkers elaborated the doctrine of the "three bodies" *(trikaya)* of the Buddha.

Mahayana thought began early on to develop the notion of a universal Buddha-nature that allowed each person the possibility of becoming a Buddha. The "three bodies" doctrine was an extension of that idea. Ultimate reality in this scheme is called the "body of cosmic law" *(dharmakaya)*, the absolute Buddha-nature, personified as the "universal Buddha" known as Vajrasattva ("thunderbolt being"). One gains access to the *dharmakaya* through wisdom. The term "body of bliss" *(sambhogakaya)* refers to the mode of being of transcendent Buddhas and *bodhisattvas* who inhabit the celestial realms. Buddhists gain access to this body through devotion. Central to the concept of the *sambhogakaya* is a pentad of Buddhas, with Vairochana, the Buddha of Infinite Light at the center, and four Buddhas at the cardinal points. Amitabha (Amida in Japan) is the best known of the four, ruling the Western paradise called the Pure Land. Kwan Yin (Kannon in Japan) is the most important of the bodhisattvas here. Through the "body of manifestation" (or transformation, *nirmanakaya*), the Buddha-nature appears among human beings, as, for example, Buddha Shakyamuni did 2,500 years ago. The Buddha teaches actively at this level and shows people the way to freedom by making concrete the ultimate reality of the *dharmakaya*. Buddhists think of the three bodies as a seamless unity.

31.   Because they consider the Buddha a historical teacher rather than a spiritual presence, do Theravada Buddhists have regular ritual practices? Are Mahayana rituals significantly different?

Many Mahayana rituals focus on devotional needs expressed as a hope for saving grace from the Buddhas and bodhisattvas. Theravada rituals, on the other hand, tend to emphasize merit making on the part of the devotee rather than access to divine power. In Thailand, an important Theravada region, lay Buddhists engage in a variety of rituals designed to ensure better karma and thus increase chances of eventual freedom from rebirth. In addition to observance of the five basic precepts enjoined on lay persons (no killing, stealing, sexual misconduct, lying, intoxicants), some still participate in the *uposatha* ("fasting"). Occurring at the four quarter-points in the lunar cycle, the observance includes a day of meditation at a local monastery. Daily feeding of monks, making offerings to a temple, joining a monastery or giving a son as a monk, and funding a new monastery are traditional activities.

Temple rituals, typically performed individually rather than communally, include offerings of flowers, fresh fruit and vegetables, and small parasols, gifts one might offer a royal person. The devotee holds a flower or candle, reverences the Buddha image by bowing, and recites prayers of praise. Especially famous temples, noted for an image such as Bangkok's Emerald Buddha, for example, become pilgrimage goals for travelers from elsewhere in the country. Some temples possess relics of the Buddha enshrined in *stupas;* devotees honor the Buddha's symbolic presence by circumambulating the reliquary. Home shrines are also used for regular morning and evening devotions. Images of the Buddha are essential in Theravada, though strictly speaking they represent the historical teacher whom devotees revere but do not worship as such. Just as an extinct fire needs no fuel, the Buddha needs no worship; ritual opens the celebrant's path toward spiritual growth. Nevertheless, popular devotion, ever immersed in concerns over controlling ubiquitous and unpredictable spirit forces, often involves invoking the spiritual aid of Buddha and of monks.

Mahayana rituals include many of the features of Theravada observance but with a different emphasis and purpose. Devotion to a personal spiritual presence and worship of a saving power are the hallmarks, and the objects of devotion include not only a number of Buddhas but a variety of *bodhisattvas* as well. Seeking other-power rather than relying on self-power, Mahayana devotees bring simple offerings not unlike those of their Theravada counterparts but add a range of chants and mantras to secure aid. A common feature is the use of large cast-metal bowls that produce a deep sustained sound when struck; meditators focus on the waning hum as a reminder of impermanence. Mahayana temples may display several Buddha images, with the central image on the altar flanked by a pair of bodhisattvas, each representing salvific power over a defined "Buddha-field." This division of spiritual labor has the effect of rendering the sources of transcendent power more approachable, especially because the bodhisattvas are by definition still lingering this side of nirvana with ears primed for the faintest call. Mahayana ritual often has a more communal feel than Theravada, with people chanting together in a large open space amid the aroma of incense.

32. Is there a Buddhist liturgical calendar? What are some of the principal Buddhist religious observances?

Timing of major Buddhist observances varies by region. Some of the more common regular observances in south Asia include the following. A three- or four-day New Year celebration in April, at the end of the dry season, witnesses a symbolic cleansing of monasteries and Buddha images, paralleling a spiritual purification of all bad karma and a renewal of Buddhist values. New Year Buddhist festivities are important all over Asia. During a full moon in May, devotees celebrate Buddha's birth, enlightenment, and death and pray for rain during the celebration of monastic ordinations. Nearly everywhere, Buddhists observe those three major events in Buddha's life, with many communities devoting separate days to each. A Buddhist "Lent" occurs during the rainy-season retreat from June to September. Young men enter monasteries for a season, devotees visit temples more often for sermons, and some add to the basic five precepts three others generally observed by monks, namely abstaining from food at certain times, reducing entertainments like movies and dancing, and refraining from the use of cosmetics. At the end of the retreat, Theravadins observe a month called Kathina, during which they increase pilgrimages and offerings.

Special days honoring bodhisattvas and saints are common in Mahayana lands. Kwan Yin is especially popular in China, and devotees observe the bodhisattva's birthday, enlightenment and nirvana, usually

on the nineteenth day of three different months. Famous founders of various lineages, such as Bodhidharma, patriarch of Ch'an, and other holy persons also have days dedicated to them in China and elsewhere. Seasonal festivities of various kinds, such as the vernal and autumnal equinoxes, are often associated with Buddhism and sometimes extend for several days before and after the seasonal event itself. Distinctive national observances, such as Japan's summer festival of the spirits of the dead, called Obon Matsuri, have sometimes been identified as Buddhist even when they originated in folk practices.

33. Statues of the Buddha so often depict him in meditation. Is meditation an important practice for Buddhists?

Meditation is arguably the most important and distinctive of all Buddhist practices, even if a relatively small percentage of even devout Buddhists manage to engage in it regularly. Meditative methods vary somewhat from one lineage or place to another, but the shared goal is either insight meditation *(vipashyana),* uncluttered penetration into the reality of the "three marks" of all existing things, impermanence, suffering, and no-soul or (less often) *dhyana,* a trancelike state. Statues of the Buddha seated in the Lotus position, with his hands palm up on his lap, fingers of the left slid under those of the right, index finger and thumb of both joined at their tips in a circle (a gesture called the *dhyani mudra*), present the ideal meditative posture. His back is nearly erect, bending very slightly at the waist, and his eyes are closed lightly or perhaps open almost imperceptibly. When Gautama sat under the bodhi tree, he was engaging in an already ancient Indian discipline aimed at "single-pointed" concentration, but the results of his practice proved to be very different from those of Jain and Hindu methods.

Although the Buddhist meditator may appear to be removed from the realities of everyday life, the actual experience of meditation requires heightened awareness of embodiment and the myriad manifestations of impermanence, death, and decay. It is almost as though one is working backward through the 12 "spokes" in the wheel of conditioned arising. Engaging in vipashyana, the meditator is able to test all inner movements on the way to more and more sustained experiences of the full awareness called nirvana. Traditional Theravada meditation typically employs no assignment of spiritual power to any being other than the meditator. That is very different from the practice of many of the Mahayana lineages, which developed their own variations on the classic method in accord with their distinctive theories of salvation. I have mentioned some of their techniques in part two above, especially those of the two main Zen lineages. A critical element in Mahayana meditation is called dwelling in tranquility *(shamatha)*. A kind of prerequisite to the analytical insight of vipashyana, it is like the clear water in which one can see the fish of insight swimming. Mahayana techniques move toward insight into the underlying reality of "emptiness" (shunyata). Some techniques are based on scripture texts (Tendai), some on repetition of mantras (Vajrayana), and some on visualization (Pure Land, Shingon, Vajrayana).

Monks and nuns in many lineages spend a great deal of their lives engaged in meditation, but there have always been provisions for lay persons to learn more-advanced techniques as well. Some people enter a monastery intending to stay for a predetermined period of months or years. Some take the occasional opportunity to make a shorter retreat in a monastery. Some temple monasteries in various countries set aside facilities for outsiders who want to meditate. In Thailand, for example, many "meditation temples" offer a variety of instructional services, levels of comfort, and degrees of involvement in monastery life, all spelled out in a guidebook published by the World Federation of Buddhists.

34. Has pilgrimage been an important practice for Buddhists?

Pilgrimage is the outward counterpart to meditation, the symbolic physical pursuit of the path to freedom. The practice of visiting Buddha's relics, including actual bodily remains as well as personal effects like his staff and bowl or footprints, began soon after his death, although pilgrimage has no explicit warrant in the Pali scriptures. Early documents say that those admitted to monastic life are "going forth" on a journey of world abandonment. Later texts have the Buddha himself enjoin pilgrimage to the places of his birth, enlightenment, first sermon, and death. India's single most popular Buddhist pilgrimage site is that of the Buddha's enlightenment at Bodhgaya, featuring Ashoka's 160-feet commemorative structure. In China, Buddhists followed the Daoist practice of designating sacred mountains. "Four famous hills," each associated with a cardinal direction, one of the four elements, and a patron bodhisattva, structure China's Buddhist landscape. In Japan, too, sacred mountains Hiei and Koya, the most famous for Buddhists, stand out on the map of pilgrimage.

As in Hindu tradition, Buddhists make pilgrimage circuits as well as visiting individual sites. On Japan's island of Shikoku, lay and monastic pilgrims still embark on the ancient 750-mile circle route with its 88 temple-stations. Pilgrims circumambulate the island, following the steps of Kukai, founder of Japan's Shingon lineage. Monks of the Tendai monasteries on Mount Hiei still make the 1,000 year-old journey of 1,000 days to sites that ring the mountain. These pilgrims don't just amble along at a leisurely pace; they maintain such a grueling clip over rugged terrain that people call them marathon monks. For these spiritual athletes, the mountain is a living mandala—a life-scale mandala that the monks literally circumambulate as opposed to a ritual model such as a scroll painting that one might meditate on and circumambulate symbolically. The journey is so arduous that they perform it in 10 terms of 100 days each, stretched out over 7 years and demanding as much as 60 miles of travel a day during the ninth term. Stations along the way include temples and shrines, tombs of holy persons associated with the Tendai lineage, and dozens of natural features such as stones, trees, and water sources. For travelers engaged in less-taxing, more-conventional types of pilgrimage, guidebooks have been a popular form of religious literature throughout the Buddhist world, covering everything from proper ritual and prayers to convenient waystations to appropriate clothing. Wherever people are free to travel, including even post-Cultural Revolution China, Buddhist pilgrims still seek the holy places.

Four:

Law and Ethics

35. Is there anything like a central teaching authority for Buddhists? Are there significant ethical differences among the various schools?

During the first generation after the death of the Buddha, the sangha was still compact enough to set its legal and ethical compass by the interpretations of the senior monks, the *thera,* and paragons of enlightenment called *arhats.* But as the community spread and more-independent monastic foundations arose across India, local discretion in implementing the rules of discipline became more accepted. Within a century or so, the first of a series of "ecumenical" councils addressed questions of accuracy in the transmission of the scriptures and various matters of monastic discipline, and their decisions had very broad authority, considering the difficulty of communication. But once Buddhist missionaries had planted the seeds of the faith in new cultural contexts at great distance, new regional authorities came into being at the more powerful monasteries.

The Buddhist university at Nalanda, in the present-day Indian state of Bihar, among others, continued to exercise a certain unifying function through education because monks returned to India from all over to study there and then return home with their new intellectual treasures. But as new lineages and subsects developed throughout Asia, teaching authority focused more and more on the founders and their successors. In time, they too tended to spin off independent foundations. In China and Japan especially, many of the major lineages became associated with a particular sacred mountain, so that the monasteries and temples located there continued to function as home base to their members. That is about as close to anything like centralized authority as one will find in Buddhist tradition today.

As a result, one can point to several notable differences in the ethical teachings of the various Buddhist lineages. Theravada ethics centers on monastic discipline with its 227 injunctions and on the responsibility of lay persons to support the sangha materially while enjoying the spiritual benefits of monastic teaching. Building on that foundation,

63

Mahayana teaching developed several distinctive themes in addition. A prominent element in Mahayana ethics is the centrality of the bodhisattva, motivated to spiritual service of humankind out of compassion. Embarking on an arduous path of discipline, the bodhisattva models all of the highest virtues or "perfections." Equally distinctive of the Mahayana ethical tradition is the notion that virtue may on occasion take priority over precept, with decision making dependent on context and on the immediate awareness and insight of the individual. It is assumed that only those well advanced in wisdom are qualified to make such delicate judgments without lapsing into sheer license or whim.

36. Is there a characteristically Buddhist moral virtue?

"Compassion *(karuna)* for all sentient beings" is the central ethical and spiritual motivation for Buddhists of virtually every lineage and school. Compassion prompted the Buddha to choose an active role as a teacher rather than keep his new enlightenment to himself. Compassion became the heart of the so-called bodhisattva career, the life of selfless service to all beings that moves individuals of the highest spiritual attainment to postpone their entry into nirvana to remain available. Critics have sometimes faulted Buddhist ethics as cool and aloof in contrast to Christianity's much more passionate divine involvement. Buddha and the bodhisattvas sacrifice little, they argue, in comparison with what Jesus suffered for redemption's sake. It is certainly true that images of the meditating and teaching Buddha communicate utter serenity, while images of the crucified Christ represent some of the most tortured and grisly religious iconography ever produced. But such criticisms are unfair and not very helpful. Although Buddhism and Christianity analyze the fundamental predicament of humanity in ways that are not so different as they might first appear, the theological functions of compassion are nevertheless different in the two traditions. Christians are called to a charity that transcends selfishness; Buddhist compassion can be authentic only if one acts out of the understanding that there is no "self" to begin with.

Buddhist compassion is devoid of egocentric clinging and possessiveness, as genuinely selfless as an ideal can be. "Tough-love" has recently become a common expression and captures something of the spirit of compassion. Some have likened Buddhist compassion to Christian *agape.* The truly compassionate person is one who is willing to do whatever is necessary to help others address the root causes of their suffering. People sometimes mistake Buddhism's call for an absolutely nonjudgmental equanimity in one's attitude toward others as a kind of cold, even elitist, distancing. In some ways Buddhist compassion is not unlike the Christian value of universal love: neither one necessarily has anything to do with "liking" the person in question.

The bodhisattva vows to place the needs of others before his or her own immediate prospects of release from suffering. But the *bodhisattva* too is the recipient of a still more ample source of kindness called the "great compassion," which is the gift of the various Buddhas. Mahayana tradition sometimes talks of a threefold combination of "kindness and compassion" *(maitri-karuna),* encompassing a basic attitude toward all beings expected of everyone; a more advanced form characteristic of bodhisattvas in the earlier phases of their moral development; and unconditional "great goodness and compassion" exercised by a Buddha. As part of their enlightenment all the Buddhas promised the possibility of that enlightenment for all devotees. All Buddhists in turn are to practice compassion wherever they encounter fundamental need.

37. Is there also a more practical side to Buddhist ethics that helps one decide how to put compassion into action?

Wisdom *(prajña)* is the other side of the coin of compassion, for one needs penetrating knowledge to channel compassion most effectively. Without wisdom, compassion is often misguided; with it, one can arrive at something like a Buddhist equivalent to natural law, insight into the way things are at their very core. An individual approaches moral effectiveness only by acquiring a deep knowledge of his or her own previous live, those of other persons as well as their future prospects, and the means to uproot the evils of sensuality, attachment, mistaken notions, and pervasive ignorance.

Combined with compassion, wisdom confers on the practitioner the virtue of skillful means *(upaya).* This means working with what one has, dealing with whatever situation arises, and turning it into a learning experience. Once there was a grieving mother who went frantically from door to door in search of someone who could revive her dead son. When she met the Buddha, she pleaded with him to work the miracle. He told her that she must first go to her village and bring back to him a sesame seed given her by a family that had never experienced death. Needless to say, she could not find such a seed, and the teacher had used her circumstances to bring home his point. Another marvelous example of the melding of wisdom and skillful means is the story of a lay Buddhist named Vimalakirti. Wearing his white garment, he went to a tavern and began to lure patrons into talking about dharma with him. Then he did the same with a prostitute, without ever revealing to her in so many words what they were discussing. Vimalakirti, the humble layman, is so resourceful that he not only puts several senior monks to shame but even teaches a pair of bodhisattvas a lesson or two. The effective teacher is like the physician who feigns death in order to persuade his stubborn sons to swallow a drug they need.

One of the most striking illustrations of skillful means is the "Parable of the Burning House" from the Lotus Sutra. A wealthy old man had a very old and once-beautiful home in which many people lived. But the house was old and in disrepair and had only one door. One day the house caught fire, and though the father detected it and escaped, he had a hard time calling his children to come out because they were absorbed in their games and unaware of the danger. So the father appealed to their desires by telling them he had a special surprise waiting for each one outside. When they all emerged unharmed, they found that he really had only one splendid cart drawn by a wondrous white ox. The father, a Buddha figure, chose to give them something far greater than they could have anticipated, enticing them from the burning house of samsara with images of lesser goods that he knew would nonetheless appeal to his children.

To sum up, in Buddhist ethics, compassion is the motive, wisdom the theoretical context and criterion for deciding the best course, and skillful means the ability to put the decision into action.

38. The "Wheel of the Law" with its eight spokes seems to be an important image for Buddhists. Why so?

Buddhism's eight-spoked Wheel of the Dharma is one of the most widely used symbols in the tradition. Even in early iconography, before artists had begun to depict the Buddha in human form, the wheel inscribed on the soles of the absent Buddha's footprints represented the Teacher. As an icon for the Eightfold Noble Path, the wheel includes all that a Buddhist needs to know and do to attain wisdom, moral conduct, and the mental discipline of absolute concentration. In the traditional breakdown of the eight steps, the concept of morality *(shila)* encompasses the third, fourth, and fifth parts: right speech, right action, and right livelihood. A kind of Buddhist "Octalogue," the path is perhaps the closest the tradition comes to an explicit code of universal conduct.

These middle three elements in the Noble Path seem very ordinary, especially when compared to the loftier goals of compassion and wisdom, but in that very ordinariness is their power. Right speech means avoiding all sins of the tongue, lying, gossip, character assassination, rudeness, and even mindless banter. Expressed positively, that means speaking purposefully, gently, and with benevolent intent. Right action means first of all doing no harm, avoiding all physical injury, sexual misconduct, and emotional or psychological exploitation. One ought also to teach by example so as to support others in their struggle to act appropriately. Right livelihood immediately rules out all means of support that may cause harm to others, especially commerce involving weapons, slavery, meat products, poisonous substances, or intoxicants. There is some leeway in these matters, so that, for example, one may eat meat that someone else has slaughtered so long as the consumer has not had it butchered explicitly for personal use. Early Buddhist teaching is very flexible and practical in matters of livelihood. One needs to be competent at a trade, avoid excessive vulnerability to loss of goods, associate with high-minded people, and live according to one's means. As part of his overall view of how one promotes ethical harmony, the Buddha even suggested that one put aside a fourth of one's income in savings, for destitution increases the potential for violence.

39. We hear a lot of talk these days about various "syndromes" allegedly responsible for the criminal actions of some individuals. What does Buddhism have to say about that sort of thing?

There is no "Twinkie Defense" in the Buddhist view of human action, no battered-child syndrome, no mitigated culpability as a result of drug-induced impairment of judgment. (I am talking here about Buddhist ethical views, not about the mechanics of any judicial system that might administer the law in countries in which Buddhism is a prominent cultural presence.) In other words, a person who is accused of first-degree murder cannot plead not guilty because he or she suffered violence as a child or because too much sugar caused temporary insanity. Buddhist ethics teaches unambiguously that each individual is always and solely responsible for his or her choices. Moral responsibility is cumulative in the sense that each person's present condition is inextricably linked with choices made in previous lives, as any future life in this world depends on choices made in this life.

From the Buddhist perspective, the judgment of a court of law is pretty much irrelevant. Punishment and retribution are inherent in the human condition. Whether or not one appears to "get away" with an essentially immoral act or with one judged illegal according to some humanly contrived set of rules, the ultimate results will be the same. What about the suffering of Job, an apparently just man who seems to get a very raw deal while apparently evil people seem to be flourishing all around him? The Judaeo-Christian response is in some ways similar to the Buddhist answer but for very different reasons. The biblical story of Job marked an important change from the view that uprightness led to reward, injustice to punishment, in this life. But Job, a righteous man, was suffering terribly. Either God was unjust, an impossible view for a person of faith, or some other law was at work, some principle of deferred retribution, perhaps. Buddhist ethics, like Judaeo-Christian ethics, teaches that sooner or later, everyone gets his or her due, regardless of what appears to be happening here and now. Legal systems can therefore only approximate authentic justice. Better to take the long view than to be depressed by any apparent failure of the "system," which, after all, is also subject to the laws of karma.

40. If Buddhists believe there is "no-self" behind the appearances of individuality, how can they talk about individual ethical responsibility?

Buddha's teaching of no-soul raises a number of important questions for ethical theory, but none quite so serious as might at first appear from the perspective of soul-based ethics. At first glance, the doctrine of no-soul seems to suggest that there is no center of consciousness and moral agency behind human actions. But the Buddha did not mean to suggest that there is "nobody home," or that human actions are merely a product of whim or chance. One measures responsibility and culpability largely in terms of the consequences or potential results of choices. To the extent that any "individual," to use conventional language, chooses to perpetuate the status quo rather than break the cycle of rebirth, responsibility accrues to that individual in the form of negative karma.

Intention is therefore the key. At the most fundamental level, all actions performed with the intent of preserving the self are unethical because they are egocentric. More broadly speaking, any action performed with any future-oriented intent will produce more of the "karmic residue" that constitutes the five aggregates we conventionally think of as a self. Right intention is the second step in the Noble Path. It presupposes that one has accepted responsibility for getting rid of all harmful views by thoroughly interiorizing the Four Noble Truths. Proper intention therefore requires that one act with no thought of selfish grasping or harm to any living thing and entirely out of benevolence. Abraham Lincoln once observed that everyone older than 40 was responsible for his or her own face. The Buddhist counterpart of that is that one cannot blame anyone else for one's intentions.

41. What is the connection between Buddhist ethics and salvation? Is there a faith–works controversy? Do Buddhists have anything similar to the concepts of *predestination* or the *will of God?*

Faith and action play somewhat different roles in the various major branches of Buddhism. For Theravada Buddhists, the closest equivalent to what Christians, for example, mean by faith is proper understanding of the Buddha's teaching. Proper knowledge or conviction has immediate consequences in the quality of one's actions, and in that sense there is no such thing as faith without good works. Among the Mahayana lineages, one finds several ways of characterizing the relationships between faith and action. Schools such as the various Zen lineages tend to be closer to the Theravada view in their ethical theories. Not only is each person ultimately responsible for his or her deeds, but the power and grace available to the various Buddhas and bodhisattvas is quite secondary to the individual's striving. Personal discipline and concentration are the first order of business. Pure Land and schools that emphasize "other-power," however, shift the focus to the transforming grace of the countless Buddhas and bodhisattvas. All one needs to do is perform the proper ritual, often involving only the repetition of a simple formula with right intent, and salvation is assured.

Predestination plays a marginal role, at most, in Buddhist teaching. Some schools teach that the power of the Buddhas and bodhisattvas is so overwhelming that all sentient beings are destined for salvation. One could theoretically thwart the greater plan with thoroughly evil intent, but the presumption remains with the infinite benefit of grace. There is a rough, but somewhat closer, analogy to the idea of God's will as expressed especially in the Christian and Islamic traditions. It is the belief in the absolute benevolence and compassion of the Buddha-nature. If there is a normative universal will, it is surely that which drives the bodhisattva to act out of compassion for all sentient beings. Aside from that, there is a dharma, an eternal law or purpose, for each individual, and every person is responsible for discovering and abiding by it.

42. How does evil manifest itself, according to Buddhist thought? Is there anything like a devil or demons?

Buddha grew up in a world of Hindu myth, populated by innumerable deities who were engaged in continuous struggle with demons. He preferred not to speculate about the existence of the gods, saying only that if they do exist, they cannot directly affect the course of the individual's religious quest for enlightenment and liberation. Neither did Buddha speculate about the existence of demonic forces, but it is interesting that a particular personification of evil does play a significant role in accounts of the Buddha's own experience. Strictly speaking, Buddhist thought has no room for the kind of mythology that is so central to Hindu tradition. Nevertheless, Buddhism did develop its brand of demonology as symbolized by Mara ("destruction, murder") and his minions. A key difference between classical Hindu thought and Buddhist thought in this respect is that in Hindu tradition, the demons tend to represent external powers, whereas Buddhist tradition internalizes them.

Mara's position in myth is that of lord of the sixth heaven in the realm of desire *(kama-dhatu)*. In the story of the Buddha, Mara attacked the meditating Siddhartha at the point of enlightenment in an attempt to dissuade him from sharing his gifts with others. Calling up first his demon hosts and then his three beautiful and seductive daughters, Mara failed to sway the Enlightened One from his mission of compassion. But in Buddhist tradition, Mara functions as a symbol of every form of ignorance that can distract one from the ultimate goal. He and his minions are personified, given mythical shape so to speak, in acknowledgement of the way that human imagination works. All temptation boils down to ignorance, but ignorance can disguise itself in countless ways to appeal to one's desires and fears. Mara therefore functions in Buddhist tradition much the way Satan does in Jesus' temptations in the wilderness.

43. Are there specific ethical expectations for monks and for lay people?

Scriptural texts collected in the Vinaya pitaka stipulate several hundred injunctions for monks and nuns, listing in detail a host of "offenses" by category. For lay persons there has never been so exhaustive a code, nor has Buddhism ever promulgated anything quite like the Judaeo-Christian "decalogue," considered divinely given commandments. Many pious lay Buddhists understand their fundamental obligations to include respect for life and refraining from lying, stealing, sexual misconduct, and intoxicating beverages. Beyond that, generosity in supplying the material needs of monks and nuns figures prominently as a universal duty. There is no doubt that monks and nuns are held to a higher standard than lay Buddhists, largely because the life of the monastic sangha affords its members greater opportunity for reflection and awareness.

Tradition lays out several clusters of precepts, numbered variously at 5, 8, 10, 250, and 348, called "the 500" in aggregate. The basic five (no killing, stealing, adultery, lying, drinking) are the minimum to ensure one's rebirth in a human realm next time around; in other words, short of this, one risks backsliding in the next life. Lay persons who wish to imitate the Buddha more closely can add three others: no cosmetics, fancy beds, or eating after noon. Theravada monks then add refraining from frivolous entertainment and from possessing luxuries to complete the first 10. Mahayana regulations modified the list for monks, shifting the emphasis, including avoidance of all unchastity, slander, insulting talk, babbling, angry outbursts, skepticism, covetousness, stealing, and lying. Some lists count 250 total rules for monks and 348 for nuns, as contained in the early Vinaya pitaka scriptures.

Monastic discipline threatens expulsion from the sangha for any of four offenses. Murder warrants a civil trial just as in the case of a lay person. If a monk kills an animal intentionally, the consequences are relatively light, by contrast, but it is assumed that the expelled monk or nun's own action will eventually be its own punishment. Unchaste behavior, even if only attempted, lands a monk or a nun on the street, as does any serious theft.

Buddhist teaching is heavily weighted to the regulation of the monastic sangha, but there is also considerable attention to the ethical needs of lay persons. Buddha recommended that lay persons provide a reasonably comfortable life for their families, short of avaricious hoarding. One should cultivate skills needed for a profession, guard the fruits of one's labor, keep the company of good people, and be frugal. Lay persons should, Buddha taught, cultivate the virtues of faith, basic morality, generosity, and wisdom. For the wealthiest lay person, Buddha recommended four kinds of happiness, including economic security, liberal spending for good purposes, freedom from debt, and, infinitely more important than the first three, living a blameless life.

44. What are some of the other principal features of Buddhist social ethics? What impact did the rejection of Hindu caste distinctions have?

Early Buddhist sources suggest that the Buddha's teaching had dramatic social consequences. He was no ivory-tower theorist but a man intent on getting at real problems. His rejection of much of traditional Indian social stratification was an important ingredient in Buddha's reformist thinking. He sought to replace the Brahmin-dominated hierarchical structure with a more egalitarian community in which power was more evenly distributed. No longer would the priests function as the unchallenged power brokers whose access to ritual mysteries made them essential gatekeepers. With his denial that the deities wielded the kind of influence needed to transform the human condition, the Buddha replaced a ritual oligarchy with a kind of relational democracy in which human beings counted, regardless of the status allotted them by the traditional system.

Buddhist community retained some very significant distinctions of seniority and gender, along with various administrative positions, but the sangha offered a drastically different model. This model included provision for the role of an enlightened ruler over society at large. It even left room for a man like Ashoka to rise to the level of the ideal monarch, a macropolitical "wheel turner" as well as a "dharma wheel turner" after the model of the Buddha himself. Realist that he was, Buddha is said to have listed 10 duties of kings, including generosity, uprightness as indicated by his practice of the first five precepts, putting the good of the people first, honesty, kindness, self-control, lack of hatred, nonviolence, patience, and willingness to govern harmoniously rather than autocratically. Some Buddhist societies even considered their rulers as bodhisattvas. One could argue that in many places, one social hierarchy merely replaced another, yielding no particular net gain, especially because Indian Buddhism seems to have put scarcely a dent in the caste arrangement. One important difference, however, was that at least in theory rulers assimilated to a Buddhist model could be held to a different and ideally higher standard. Though the broader ideal of a global community that is able to transcend national and ethnic boundaries has remained largely elusive, Buddhists active in social concerns all over Asia have continued to challenge the monastic establishment's lack of involvement in society's most pressing concerns.

45. I recall how during the Vietnam war some Buddhist monks doused themselves with gasoline and died in protest of the war. Does Buddhism condone suicide?

Buddhist teaching forbids suicide outright in its disciplinary codes, but some classic texts appear to allow some latitude in interpreting certain types of self-immolation as a symbolic expression of universal compassion. Buddha himself encountered a tradition of death by fasting among Hindus and Jains but ruled it out for himself and his disciples. Several of the *Jatakas,* stories of previous lives of the Buddha-to-be, suggest that a bodhisattva might risk life and limb for the good of others, and at least one Mahayana sutra tells how in a previous life the Buddha sacrificed himself to feed a starving tiger. In Japan the practice of ritual suicide called *seppuku* was sometimes associated with Zen by way of the samurai code but was generally motivated by a desire for a heroic death rather than out of religious altruism.

Perhaps the most significant text appears in the Lotus Sutra, in a chapter that describes events in two previous lives of a bodhisattva. He decides that the most fitting way to reverence the Buddha and his dharma is to prepare his body with incense and flower oils for 12 centuries and then burn himself. For another 1,200 years his body burned, and he was reborn as a disciple of the Buddha. But when the Buddha died, the bodhisattva could think of no better offering than to burn his own arms in homage before the 84,000 stupas bearing the Buddha's relics. His wisdom and virtue caused his arms to regenerate, but the story is still quite shocking. Other texts also speak of bodhisattvas offering body parts to the fire of self-sacrifice. Furthermore, according to ancient tradition, the most accomplished meditators generate such heat through ascetic practice that they illuminate the world like a blazing fire. The Vietnamese monks who burned themselves during the war, at least some of whom were from a Zen monastery, may have drawn their motivation from such scriptural recommendations of self-sacrifice as the perfect form of generosity. By their conflagration, both spiritual and physical, they sought to call attention to the suffering of their brothers and sisters in the hope of mitigating it.

In summary, suicide motivated merely by a craving to be relieved of bodily suffering does not liberate but only condemns one to be reborn and face the same craving again. In the case of the very rare person who is truly free from ignorance and inordinate cravings, suicide might be an acceptable choice in the event, for example, of terminal illness or an extraordinary need to bring to center stage the plight of a segment of humanity.

FIVE:

SPIRITUALITY

46. What do you mean by the term *spirituality* in relation to Buddhism? If there is no "spirit," how can there be spirituality?

Buddhism's doctrine of no-soul might appear at first to be quite incompatible with commonly accepted notions of spirituality, but only if one takes the doctrine literally. Buddha certainly emphasized the primacy of experience and taught a way to refine one's understanding of human relationships to an ultimate reality, even when the tradition does not describe that reality as divine. All traditions of spirituality focus on the experiential aspects of religious belief and practice, and in that sense Buddhist teaching represents a very high level of spirituality.

Buddhist sources reveal a wide range of experiential and relational themes. The earliest scriptures connect Buddhists to fundamental aspects of the founder's spirit and legacy. Theravada texts emphasize the Buddha's role as historical teacher and exemplar. Mahayana texts elaborate on the transcendent saving grace of the innumerable beings who manifest the Buddha-nature. Through prayer and ritual, Buddhists express devotion variously in profound reverence for the Teacher and in supplication for a savior's attentiveness and powerful presence. Sources of practical inspiration also provide believers concrete examples of high values and commitment in legends of holiness such as arhats, important founders of religious orders, and lay Buddhists of extraordinary virtue.

Aesthetic values also play an important role in the tradition. Visual arts and architecture communicate aspects of the mood and feel of Buddhist spirituality that words alone cannot contain. The great temples often breathe an air of meditative calm, and images of the Buddha invite contemplation. In addition Buddhists have expressed their deepest values through various forms of community and institutional structures, the most important being the monastic sangha. For members of the larger community whose chosen way of life offers them the luxury of total dedication to the interior journey, Buddhist tradition supplies enormous resources in the form of advanced spiritual pedagogy in the more refined teachings and demanding disciplines. Finally, Buddhist religious literature also includes the testimony of personal experience in the diaries and other first person accounts of those who have struck out on the path before. Their stories offer both encouragement and occasional cautionary tales for fellow seekers.

47.   What does faith mean to Buddhists? What is it they believe in?

A merchant from a Chinese town decided he would travel to India in search of goods. Word got around among his neighbors, and a devout old woman asked if the merchant would do her a favor that would make her very happy. She wanted him to bring back for her a tooth of the Buddha. As he set off on his long journey, the merchant promised he would fulfill her desire. Months later the merchant was nearing the end of his trip. His town came into view down the road and he rejoiced to be home. Suddenly he remembered his promise to the old woman and realized that he had neglected his vow. Just then he spied a dead dog by the roadside and decided he would pluck out one of its teeth. He wrapped the tooth in a cloth and presented it to the woman. With great delight and ceremony, she enshrined the tooth lovingly in her home and began to spread the news that she had the wondrous relic. Soon pilgrims began to come from afar to visit the shrine. The tooth began to glow, growing in brightness until the woman's whole house was illumined. Smitten with guilt, the merchant decided he must at last tell the truth. He confessed his deception to the old woman and begged forgiveness. Undeterred, she insisted that he must be mistaken: One had only to look to see how the tooth enlightened all.

The story makes several important points but from a decidedly Mahayana perspective. Faith and devotion yield amazing results. One might even say that belief is so powerful that it can transform even the humblest, most defiled bit of refuse into a sacred memento. Right view is, after all, the first step on the Eightfold Path. On the other hand, the story also reinforces the notion that nothing material is inherently significant. Strictly speaking and from a Theravada point of view, one ought never to arrive at the point of being so invested in any mere material traces as to have that investment blind one to the basic facts. But because Buddhism is such a diverse phenomenon, there are many ways of understanding religious belief and commitment.

The most commonly used and closest Buddhist equivalent to "faith" is *shraddha,* which actually means something more like a confidence that arises from conviction. Popular usage has associated the term with devotion, but its more basic meanings are linked to becoming convinced about a given state of affairs. It can also connote the experience of joy when one becomes aware of goodness and a desire to pursue a particular goal. The conviction at the core of shraddha is akin to what happens when one "sees" that something one has been told actually is the case. In that sense, Buddhist "faith" is very unlike the classic Christian notions of either assent to a mysterious truth or acquiescence in the truth of an assertion that one cannot prove but which is part of tradition. *Shraddha* is the first of four virtues likely to assure a lay Buddhist's happiness (followed by morality, generosity, and wisdom).

Buddhist faith "sees" that the Buddha, dharma, and sangha (the Three Refuges) are worthy goals and hold the answer to the fundamental human dilemmas. Faith is therefore the ability to penetrate beneath appearances to the underlying reality of one's experience, the dispelling of illusion, and a profound insight into the impermanence, suffering, and absence of soul that are the true characteristics of existence. Faith implies the freedom of gradually sloughing off the bondage of anxiety for self-preservation.

48. Most images of Buddha and the bodhisattvas seem peaceful and approachable, but in a museum recently I saw a figure engulfed in flames, with a penetrating gaze. The label identified the figure as Japanese Buddhist. What is this unnerving presence doing in Buddhist garb?

As in virtually every spiritual tradition, Buddhist interpretations of the mysteries of ultimate reality and of the human psyche are full of surprises. Sweetness and light, serenity and benevolence are only part of the story. Sooner or later, one has to confront the demons and deal with the less consoling side of mystery. More than likely, the character you saw was one of the "Kings of Knowledge" *(vidyarajas),* five tough customers who guard their quarters of cosmic turf with grim efficiency. They are wrathful emanations of the five universal Buddhas, also known as *jinas* or conquerors by virtue of their enlightenment, who reign at the center and at the four cardinal points of the universe (as in the *trikaya* discussed in section three). Each of these "great and venerable kings of mystic knowledge," as they are known in Japan, also enjoys the service of a coterie of acolytes. In addition to the five kings, a host of other "terrible" deities represent the wrathful aspect of the various bodhisattvas. Historically, these figures made their way into China as variations of wrathful Hindu deities and were incorporated into the more esoteric Buddhist schools, especially Chen-yen and its Japanese branch, called Shingon.

Buddhism's fearsome five and their colleagues look and sound like the very essence of anger, but they do not broadcast their fury indiscriminately. They embody the fierce concentration and uncompromising determination required for victory over inappropriate craving. In their anger, they gather the distillate potency of mantras and embody a kind of psychic projection of the power every devotee must summon up to overcome spiritual challenges. The kings therefore inspire actual terror only in those unwilling to grapple with the roots of evil. For serious seekers, they are actually a reassuring presence. Though images of one or another of the kings frequently appear alone in museums, in their ritual settings they are typically grouped together and surrounded by a veritable cloud of intimidating minions.

My personal favorite, and the one you are most likely to have seen in the museum, is Fudo Myo-o. Destroyer of the craving that causes suffering, this "Immutable Lord" is the piqued side of Vairochana, Buddha of the Sun who reigns at the center of the cosmos. With the sword in his right hand, he dispatches the three passions of ignorance, greed, and anger; with the lasso in his left, he restrains evil powers. Fudo prolongs by a half-year the lives of his devotees, allowing them extra time to overcome any remaining barriers to spiritual freedom now and thus obviate the need for rebirth. With the assistance of his eight acolytes, disgruntled children all, Fudo Myo-o also quells the demons responsible for disease. Though he and the other kings were originally associated with esoteric sects, they have become very popular in other lineages, including that of Nichiren. If looks could kill, many an art lover would have left the local museum's Asian gallery feet first. Fortunately for all concerned, the kings of knowledge are angry purely out of compassion.

49. Many traditions of spirituality devise systematic analyses of spiritual progress. Does Buddhism have anything like that?

For a tradition whose founder repudiated formalism and systematic structures, Buddhism gave rise to an astounding array of typologies of the spiritual life. From carefully elaborated steps in meditative practice to

levels of advancement along the Middle Path to stages of higher pedagogy, Buddhist teaching offers a method for analyzing every imaginable
nook and cranny of the spiritual cosmos. It all begins with interpretations
of the Buddha, who modeled an aspect of spiritual attainment suited to
seekers at every level of aptitude and commitment. For the lay person, he
was the paradigm of striving embodied in the bodhisattva. For monks and
nuns, the Buddha modeled the ideal of the arhat, one who has attained a
high level of perfection. For the most advanced, he was the "perfect
gainer of enlightenment"; as such he modeled simultaneously (here in
ascending order) the "humble listener" *(shravaka)* who attains the goal
by hearing the dharma but does not show the path to others; the "solitary
enlightened one" *(pratyekabuddha)* who attains something less than perfect enlightenment on his own but does not teach others; and the person
who both attains perfect enlightenment without a teacher and shows others the path *(samyaksambuddha)*. Buddha's own life experience thus
makes him all things to all seekers.

Theravada tradition lays out a series of gradations along the path
to the status of arhat, one who attains enlightenment. Those who have
accomplished the most rudimentary purification from the world's defile-
ments are called the ones "immersed in water" (*sotapanna,* "stream-
winner"). A notch above them are the "still-returning" *(sakadagamin)*
individuals who had further reduced their defilement but remain likely
to backslide into immersion in worldly affairs. A complete purification
from defilement characterizes the "nonreturner" *(anagamin)* who is no
longer subject to reimmersion. Finally, the arhat is one who arrives at
final attainment of nirvana (with remainder).

A range of spiritual disciplines provide not only the preferred
methods for achieving advanced levels of development but gauges for
measuring one's progress. Sometimes the tradition offers lists of critical
ingredients in the quest for one's goal, not as rungs on a ladder but as
qualities of equal importance to be cultivated simultaneously. So, for
example, the "seven factors of enlightenment" include mindfulness,
investigation, energy, joy, relaxation, concentration, and equanimity.
These are not so much causes as touchstones of enlightenment. Other
clusters are more developmental and sequential. Here are two examples
that point out important differences of emphasis that characterize Theravada and Mahayana approaches.

Theravada teacher Buddhaghosa's scheme prescribes meditation on the "seven purities" (of virtue, mind, view, overcoming doubt, insight into right and wrong, insight into progress, and of knowledge and insight themselves) that leads to the state of "fruition," in which the mind is free of objects, and finally to the "cessation of thought and feeling," nirvana this side of death.

Perhaps the most famous of these schemata is associated with the so-called "Ox-herding Pictures" of Zen, a series of charming and evocative images illustrating essential steps toward freedom. Searching (1) for the ox (a symbol of ultimate reality), the seeker discovers (2) its footprints. In the distance he spies the ox (3) and manages to catch it (4). After taming the beast (5), the careful seeker rides it home (6). After a while he forgets about the ox (7), aware only of self, eventually forgetting self as well (8). Aware in silence of the emerald water and the indigo mountain (9), the seeker finds himself once again in the world where all who meet him benefit from his enlightenment (10).

50. Is there a tradition of Buddhist spiritual direction?

Various forms of spiritual direction are among the standard methods of several Buddhist lineages, but the practice is often quite different from the kind of conversational exchange or pastoral counseling that many Christians associate with the term. A good example of one approach is that of Dogen (1200–1253), founder of the Soto Zen lineage in Japan. Dogen believed that individuals who are capable of achieving enlightenment alone are exceedingly rare. Most people need assistance in interpreting the "80,000 phenomena" in the external world that inevitably figure in the arising of the desire for enlightenment in the first place.

Not just any master *(roshi)* will do. Better not to study the dharma at all than to attempt it with the wrong guide. Dogen describes his own frustration in the search for the right teacher. Too many were green wood, or sought to understand the source of a stream by examining a handful of water or the roots of a tree by observing its branches, or were too in love with the sound of their own voices. The guide treats the male disciple like a son, warmly but firmly, after the model of the Buddha himself. A worthy master remains humble enough even to seek his monks' forgiveness of his faults. Most of all the authentic master lives as he speaks.

An aspirant must be docile and of even temper, ready to abandon personal views when experience proves them inadequate, but not too ready to give undue credence to those of another, even a master of great antiquity. Let the seeker receive the master's guidance as though it were water poured from one vessel into another. A master is like a potter molding clay. Some conflict, however, is inevitable and even necessary in transmission of the dharma; the "vines" of doctrinal entanglement help master and disciple grow together. Dogen insisted that study of the sutras was integral to the process, combining intellectual content with personal encounter. Individual meetings between disciple and master typically occurred briefly each morning during most of the year, but during extended meditation sessions *(sesshin)*, they might meet twice; during the seven day "great meditation" *(dai-sesshin),* as many as four times daily, to discuss the disciple's views on his koan.

When the master's bell rings, signaling time for interview *(sanzen),* monks who want to see him line up single file outside his room. Interaction is sometimes vigorous, a harsh word, a shout, a monk chased away by an angry roshi. Senior monks sometimes urge juniors who haven't visited the master recently to take their responsibility more seriously and may occasionally drag a slacker bodily to see the master. Just as at a certain moment hen and chick begin to tap the shell simultaneously from without and within, master and disciple know intuitively decisive events in the disciple's life. Dogen used the koan not to negate reason (as the Rinzai lineage tends to do) but as a parable or allegory, acknowledging that language has symbolic value as a means toward the goal of enlightenment.

51. Are there any figures in Buddhist spirituality like Christian saints?

Embodiments or personifications of sanctity take a variety of forms in the different branches of Buddhism. Theravada teaching extols the arhat as the pinnacle of holiness. Achieving the ultimate goal of liberation by his own effort, the arhat models the Buddha's example of self-reliance most of all. Strictly speaking anyone can achieve this exalted status, but the path is so arduous that tradition acknowledges only a handful apart from the early disciples of the Buddha.

Among the most celebrated arhats are the "five hundred" who are said to have attended the first Buddhist council. This canonically recognized gathering forms an interesting bridge between Theravada and Mahayana lineages in that, even though the Chinese and Japanese schools do not share the Theravada regard for the reclusive arhat as a living ideal, they do revere these historic companions of the Buddha. Chinese Mahayana lore even attributes immortality to the *lohan* (Chinese for arhat), often in groups of 18, teaching that they are spiritually present with their disciples and are especially associated with sacred mountains. A distinctive hagiography preserves stories of the previous lives of the lohans as examples fit for meditation. There is also a distinctive iconography, typically depicting the holy one in monk's robes, with the elongated ears associated with the Buddha, seated in the lotus position, usually with eyes open, sometimes with a scroll or other sign of teaching authority, sometimes rapt in meditation.

Chinese and Japanese tradition have extended the category further by acknowledging a number of Ch'an masters as lohans (*rakan* in Japanese). Founding figures, such as the Ch'an patriarch Bodhidharma, have taken their place among the ranks of lohans as well. Even Marco Polo made his way into the Chinese communion of saints. Japanese patriarchs of the Tendai and Shingon lineages, Saicho and Kukai, as well as the founders (and often their successors) of other denominations such as Nichiren, Honen, and Shinran, are revered much the way Christians revere patron saints. Statues and painted portraits of them are among the art treasures of the various lineages.

In Tibetan Buddhism, several lineages of *tulkus* ("transformation body," reincarnation of a deceased individual), as embodied in the various lamas ("none above," guru) definitely fall in this category. Magical or miraculous powers are sometimes attributed to these human beings in whom a special manifestation of the Buddha-nature resides. Unlike Christian saints they do not, with the exception of the Tibetan *tulkus,* undergo a defined regimen of scrutiny as prerequisite to their being acclaimed worthy of reverence.

Finally, bodhisattvas are very important mediating figures in nearly all the Mahayana lineages. As an ideal of holiness, the bodhisattva represents a much more engaged service to humankind than the arhat. Theoretically any human being can become a bodhisattva, but because the "career" or pedagogy such a transformation requires is so demanding, a relatively few historical figures have been so identified. Tibet's Dalai Lamas are unusual in that they have nearly all been considered reincarnations of the bodhisattva Avalokiteshvara. Most are mythical or entirely legendary figures whose whole reason for being is to hand their own infinite merit over to suffering souls who need it desperately.

52. Could you say more about the role of *bodhisattvas?*

According to Mahayana teaching, a bodhisattva ("enlightenment being") is any person who has achieved enlightenment but chooses to postpone entry into nirvana and remain involved in the realm of suffering out of compassion for all sentient beings. This is clearly an extraordinarily altruistic option, motivated by the conviction that all beings are potential Buddhas. A bodhisattva undergoes a rigorous ten-stage spiritual discipline toward the immediate goal of combining compassion with wisdom. Beginning with a vow *(pranidhana)* to achieve enlightenment and to lead all others toward that goal, the aspirant moves initially through the first six "Lands" *(bhumi)* or stages, each of which is associated with a specific "perfection" *(paramita,* "that which has attained the far shore"). Generosity is associated with the land of joy, self-discipline with the land of purity. In the land of radiance, the aspirant gains patience through the understanding of impermanence and is rid of desire, anger, and ignorance. Conferring the virtue of exertion or vigor, the "blazing land" burns away residual misunderstanding and confers wisdom. In the land called "extremely difficult to conquer," the traveler gains proficiency in meditation and penetrates the Four Noble Truths. Wisdom, the realization of reality as emptiness, comes in the "land in view of wisdom." Up to this point, the aspirant is still at risk of slipping back, still an earthly bodhisattva.

Here the traveler could choose to enter nirvana. Opting to serve others, the bodhisattva, fully worthy of the name at this point, needs four further perfections that mark the transition to the status of transcendent bodhisattva, to be reborn in a special way that makes a salvific role possible. In the "far-going" land, skill-in-means is the reward, along with the ability to be manifest in all shapes. Gaining beneficence in the "immoveable" land and now aware of details of his or her own future buddhahood, the bodhisattva begins to bestow merit on the suffering. Granted the certainty that all gains are now permanent, the bodhisattva in the land of "good thoughts" attains the perfection of wisdom that prevents the memory of ignorance and suffering from causing the slightest disturbance. Overflowing with compassion, the traveler arrives finally at the land of the "clouds of dharma," immersed in perfect understanding, and rains down the Good Law like a saturated cloud. At this point, but one further step remains to Buddhahood, but the bodhisattva will wait, forever if necessary.

53. Is there such a thing as Buddhist mysticism?

If we define *mysticism* generally as the encounter with mystery and the meditative or contemplative experience of realities beyond the ordinary, then we can definitely speak of Buddhist mysticism. Because traditional Buddhist psychology denies the existence of a substantial self or ego (the doctrine of *anatman*), mystical experience can not be a question of either union of two "personal" entities or even of "loss of self" in a greater, oceanic reality such as we find variously in Hindu, Christian, or Islamic mystical sources. The Hindu mystic typically seeks realization of the oneness of the self (atman) with the ultimate reality (Brahman), a unity that already exists and of which the seeker must become aware. For most Christian mystics, the goal is loving union of the soul with God, and Muslim mystics talk of loss of individuality in the sea of divine mercy. From the Buddhist perspective, there is nothing to join and nothing to lose. What's left then? What else could possibly "happen" to a mystic?

Realization of the simple "suchness" of whatever is. That is the goal. I earlier nominated the concept of *emptiness* as arguably the most distinctively Buddhist description of reality, and it is surely the key characteristic of Buddhist mysticism. Scholars frequently speak of the Buddhist mysticism of emptiness and then strive at great length to fill in the blank, so to speak. Emptiness is intimately connected to the teaching of nonsoul or egolessness, and when a Buddhist meditates, that truth is ever the focus of concentration, the "something" at the heart of nothing. Theravadins meditate on the various reminders of impermanence and on the insubstantiality of even the dharma itself. Mahayana Buddhists have evolved theories and methods varying from one lineage to another.

Recall, for example, the ox-herding pictures. The point at which the seeker forgets both self and ox is symbolized by an empty circle, the eighth picture. But how can one concentrate on nothing? How can "nothing" yield insight? And into what? Talk of emptiness is in fact a way to get a grip on everything that is, by accepting all things in their utter simplicity. The Buddhist mystic is, paradoxically, the most firmly rooted of all persons by virtue of maximum freedom from attachment to particularity. All things and persons are able to be just what they are, unspoiled by any meanings or judgments imposed by the mystic. Two more images remain beyond the eighth ox-herding picture. One does not merely float off into the empty circle, never to be heard from again. Buddhist mysticism has a strong ethical thrust that reinserts the meditator into the ordinary, both as one now capable of truly enjoying the arresting "suchness" of all things and as one moved by compassion to share the insight with others.

54. Does asceticism have an important place in Buddhist spirituality?

One of Buddha's earliest realizations was that extremes of any kind, whether toward hedonism or toward self-denial, produce no benefit. Tradition says that the once spoiled-rotten rich kid swung so far the other way that he nearly perished, a bag of skin and bone scarcely able to sit up. As every stage of the Eightfold Path indicates, he emphasized "right and proper" measure in all things. Measured discipline, a genuine "middle way," appears to have been uppermost in the Teacher's mind. As in virtually every major religious tradition, however, there are numerous Buddhist examples of unimaginable austerity in the name of spiritual growth. There have been wandering ascetics unattached to monasteries, but even in community, monastic members of the sangha focus on personal questing. Theravada Buddhism's notion of the arhat as the spiritual ideal suggests a strong emphasis on aloofness from human contact, on going it alone like a solitary rhinoceros, well armored against external threat.

Mahayana schools have their forms of asceticism as well. Monastic disciplines common to nearly all branches of Buddhism include restricted sleep and food, simplicity in clothing and physical surroundings, and limited interaction with fellow monks or nuns. The discipline of begging food remains a symbolically important practice, calculated to foster humility rather than to offset actual poverty. Meditative practice is perhaps the most important of all ascetical disciplines; it requires immense patience, mental endurance, and the ability to brush aside simple distractions and the discomfort of protracted stillness.

Tibetan tradition uses the term *mahasiddha* ("great spiritual achiever") to refer to an individual who has fully integrated the teachings of the tantras ("continuum," "manual," "system"), scriptural texts of varying degrees of difficulty that focus on controlling inner experience for spiritual purposes. Much of the symbolism is sexual, leading to the goal of transcending the male–female polarity in the perfect melding of wisdom and compassion. A technique that the Buddha would likely find extreme is the tantric use of sexual intercourse in connection with meditation. The idea is to so deny one's natural responses as to prevent ejaculation by returning the semen to its source at the last moment. Tantric practices have, understandably, been subject to abuse, but the goal is transcendence. Tibetan Buddhists also revere a group of 84 *mahasiddhas,* slightly less unorthodox than their tantric counterparts.

Finally, it is essential to keep in mind that all Buddhist ascetical disciplines are meant to serve one purpose, the full realization of the Four Noble Truths. The first step is surely the most demanding of all, namely the determination to banish all forms of denial and deal with the bare facts of one's experience with brutal honesty.

55. Are there distinctively Buddhist views about sacred space? About sacred time?

Traditional (especially Mahayana) Buddhist views of the structure of the spiritual cosmos divide it into three realms, that of desire *(kama-dhatu),* form *(rupa-dhatu),* and nonform *(arupa-dhatu).* But the tripartite world this model describes is at least as much metaphysical as physical. When combined with the metaphor of the two shores—this shore of ignorance and the other of enlightenment—and the two levels of experience—the endless rebirth of samsara and the liberation of nirvana—the spiritual cosmos looks like this: At the lowest level, the realm of desire and greed, dwell those who have no positive spiritual aspirations, no desire to set out for the far shore, because they lack even the rudiments of wisdom. Theirs is a world haunted by demons and in the grip of death. On the next level, the realm of form, dwell in those who have begun to move toward the first two steps on the Eightfold Path (right beliefs and resolve) and are aware of the need to seek a higher rebirth through better karma; they remain, however, aware largely of life as a this-worldly matter and so are still immersed in a world of appearances.

At the next level, the realm of nonform, are those who have become accomplished in the middle stages of the path. They have risen to a higher level of morality and have learned to transcend the realm of form by living lives of right speech, right action, and right livelihood. Still on "this" shore and bound up in samsara, these seekers are nevertheless progressing in spiritual realization and freedom from external appearances. Traditional accounts typically associated this level with monastic members who have advanced through the first six stages of the bodhisattva path. Like those at the lower level, the quality of their actions assures them of a better rebirth.

But there remains a level beyond the realm of nonform, that of nirvana, which is beyond both form and formlessness. This level is the equivalent of heaven, the other shore, a land no longer profane but purely sacred. Here dwell the Buddhas and heavenly bodhisattvas and potentially others who have reached the perfection of "concentration" *(samadhi)* characterized by right energy, right concentration, and right absorption, the last three stages on the Eightfold Path. Perhaps the finest visual expression of this image of the spiritual universe is the Great Stupa at Barabudur in central Java (Indonesia). Built around 800, the massive structure is a nine-level stone itinerary of the Mahayana pilgrimage. Circumambulating the structure clockwise, the pilgrim "meditates" physically. Moving around the four sides of the realm of desire, the pilgrim ponders stone reliefs illustrating the law of karma, of cause and effect. Walking up steps to the second terrace, the pilgrim enters the realm of form. Circumambulating terraces two through five, the meditator contemplates reliefs of the life of the historical Buddha, his previous lives in scenes from the *Jatakas,* and images of future Buddhas and bodhisattvas. The sixth terrace, still square, marks the transition to the realm of nonform. Three further circular terraces offer the meditator only small hollow stupas with slatwork openings through which the pilgrim can catch just a glimpse of a Buddha image. At the summit and center of Barabudur is a massive solid stupa, intentionally left unfinished but containing a hidden image of the central Buddha, representing nirvana.

Sacred time in Buddhist tradition has three especially important points of reference. First, of course, there is the life of the historical

Buddha with the various major events celebrated on the annual liturgical calendar. Second, the previous lives of the Buddha as told in the *Jataka* tales represent the uninterrupted presence of the Enlightened One in a saving role among humankind. Finally, there is the time between one's own present life and the eventual achievement of freedom from rebirth. For those who arrive at that point, time ceases.

Six:

Buddhism and the Humanities

56. Is there such a thing as Buddhist theology?

Earliest Buddhist teaching was clearly nontheistic. The Buddha had grown up in a world permeated by Hindu god–talk and was apparently aware of at least the fundamentals of Hindu theology. He nevertheless refused to speculate or talk about the gods in any way that might short-circuit the process of seeking the truth through experience. Several of the Buddha's disciples tried to engage him in theological discussion. He replied consistently that he would neither deny nor affirm the existence of the deities, for such speculative talk was futile and a distraction from more pressing concerns. If the gods did exist, he suggested, however potent they might be, they could not "save" anyone from the duty to seek enlightenment. If *theology* means what human beings understand and say about God, strictly speaking there is no Buddhist theology.

Nevertheless, even in the early Buddhist texts, one finds a good deal of material analogous to early Christian religious and theological literature. Buddhaghosa (fl. c. 400), whose name means something like "Voice of Enlightenment," was one of the most important exponents of Theravada doctrine. Playing a role perhaps comparable to that of Augustine in Christianity, Buddhaghosa set out to reflect on a wide range of religious issues "in view of nirvana" as Saint Augustine had "in view of eternity." Focusing on methods designed to help the aspirant stay fixed on the goal of enlightenment, Buddhaghosa has recourse to striking imagery, even recommending meditation on the corruption of the body in death as a way of shocking oneself out of attachment to life in this world. At the heart of his work is detailed analysis of the practice of insight meditation (vipashyana), an almost universal phenomenon in Buddhist thought. Buddhaghosa's *Path of Purity (Visuddhimagga)* is an important elaboration of early Buddhist doctrine.

Mahayana developments in Buddhology and soteriology move a step closer to truly theological literature. Many Asian Buddhists would find it easy enough to call the various Buddhas deities, and Mahayana cosmology and eschatology are replete with Hindu divine personages and talk of realms of reward and punishment beyond this world.

Arguably, Mahayana's first major theological writer was Ashvaghosa (fl. c. 100), a convert from Hinduism. His two most influential works were a Sanskrit drama, the first complete life of the Buddha, rich in the devotional imagery that came to typify Mahayana theology; and a religious epic poem whose hero, Nanda, the Buddha himself teaches to renounce the world. So great was Ashvaghosa's stature that later tradition attributed to him a much later work entitled the *Treatise on the Awakening of Mahayana Faith.*

57. Have Buddhists developed a significant literature in philosophy?

Many commentators have argued that Buddhism is not a religion at all, but a philosophical tradition. While I would defend Buddhism as an authentic religious tradition, there is no doubt that some of its most influential writings have been philosophical. Buddha himself breathed the air of the Upanishads' philosophical theology, and his earliest teaching responded to some Upanishadic themes, but he was primarily a practical man who wanted nothing to do with idle speculation. The first genuinely philosophical literature appears in the Pali Canon's Abhidharma ("superior doctrine") Pitaka, with its detailed analyses of central themes contained in the earlier two "baskets" of the Pali Canon. Early scholar–monks emphasized the importance of key concepts of the primitive dharma. But not many generations along, a school of lay Buddhists developed a body of literature around the "perfection of wisdom" (prajñaparamita), rejecting Abhidharma's teaching as contrary to the spirit of the Buddha. That school in turn became the impetus for two of the most important schools of religious philosophy, the Madhyamika and the Yogacara.

A south Indian Buddhist named Nagarjuna (fl. c. 200) founded a school called Madhyamika, "Followers of the Middle Path." He was one of the foremost proponents of the concept of *emptiness* (shunyata) in relation to the 12 stages of dependent coorigination often referred to as the wheel of becoming. According to Nagarjuna's doctrine of bilevel truth, one can use conventional language to describe only a sliver of the ultimate truth, which eludes all language. All dharma, therefore, merely alludes to distant realities and is empty in itself. Nagarjuna's most important contribution was his critique of the various "realist" teachings of both Hindu and Buddhist philosophy that all rational concepts correspond to substantial physical realities. To use a contemporary expression, he "deconstructed" Indian philosophy by arguing that human beings confer meaning and even "being" itself on the objects of our experience. Nagarjuna's views made a very sophisticated and important contribution to religious epistemology. Translated into Tibetan and Chinese, Nagarjuna's originally Sanskrit works formed the nucleus of an early lineage called the "Three Treatise School" in both China and Japan.

Two fourth–fifth century Indian brothers, Vasubandhu and Asanga, were the major contributors to the Yogacara school, also known as the *Vijñanavada* ("consciousness-doctrine"). They employed a systematic approach to yogic discipline to peel away the various layers of consciousness that human beings mistake for external reality. The goal is to correct the mistaken belief that "what I think" is identical with "what is really out there." The heart of the matter is that all human consciousness is itself dependent on still more elusive realities and is therefore not a dependable index of reality. Realization of this radical "emptiness" of human consciousness leads to genuine freedom from the tyranny of self-deceit. Yogacara thought, like Madhyamika, made its way into China and Japan and survives most notably in the small Japanese Hosso lineage.

58. Most people consider the pagoda a characteristic form of Buddhist architecture. How did that develop?

Buddhism's most important early structures are stone-clad commemorative earthen mounds called stupas. Atop the solid hemispheric body sits a solid box crowned by a shaft through a series of three disks that yield a conical profile like that of an evergreen tree. According to legend, the Buddha instructed his followers as to what to do with his remains by overturning his begging bowl and placing his staff and folded garments on top. Originally used as repositories for relics of the Buddha, the early stupas were simple earthworks with a minor superstructure that offered just a hint of upward movement. As a symbol of the earthly Buddha whose legacy was his teaching, the stupa spread rapidly with missionaries to central, east, and Southeast Asia. Miniaturized stupas in wood and metal became popular as portable reliquaries, and small stone stupas began to appear in clusters along pilgrim roads, marking spots for rest and devotion.

Gradually builders and artists began to refine and streamline the primitive stupa form, redefining the relationships among its basic elements,

which when seen from above (or in "plan") are a square base, a circular body, a square cap, and a circular spire (the very same succession of symbolic shapes that appear in many mandalas). Viewed from the side (or in "elevation"), the base gained height, the body stretched upward much the way a clay ball rises as a potter spins it into a vase, the square cap became a rectangle, and the treelike spire became taller and acquired more disks, up to as many as 13. This peculiar development continued until eventually the base, the body, and the cap became so attenuated that only the multitiered spire remained, almost as though a woodworker had put a stupa on a lathe and turned it till it became a graceful knurled post.

In China architects translated the solid upright form of the spire with its multiple circular tiers into a multilevel reliquary structure called the pagoda, evidently a corruption of the term *dagoba* originally used in Sri Lanka to refer to the upper part of the stupa. Now one could actually enter the ground floor where relics of the Buddha and other holy figures were kept. As Buddhism moved into Korea and Japan, the shape of the pagoda's plan changed from circular to polygonal to square and the number of roof levels decreased. Most full-scale Japanese pagodas, for example, have 5 square-roofed levels, with 3 and 7 the commonest variations, while miniatures often retain as many as 13 tiers.

The evolution from stupa to pagoda offers a fascinating visual parallel to developments in Buddhist soteriology. From the Theravada emphasis on the humanity of the Buddha who taught by example, to the various Mahayana teachings about multiple saving Buddhas and bodhisattvas inhabiting countless levels of the cosmos, the transformation of a ponderous earth shape into one that reaches for the heavens illustrates a Buddhist theological tale of an increasingly transcendent reality. In fact, as if the multitiered pagoda's were not sufficiently vertical, many are also topped by a brand new spire complete with 9, 11, or 13 remnants of the ancient stupa's parasols, transcendence piled upon transcendence.

59. What other architectural types have Buddhists developed for religious purposes?

Pagodas are the most visible of several important Buddhist architectural developments. Temple complexes, often associated with monastic residential facilities, have included various types of religious structures based on the functional requirements of Buddhist communities. Let me describe some of the main features of these complexes in China and Japan, keeping in mind that one can only suggest the overall outlines of a very diverse phenomenon. Early Chinese monastery–temples were modeled on secular designs such as the palace; only the pagoda represented a uniquely Buddhist structure. Chinese and Japanese complexes typically feature a large courtyard defined by an enclosure that is lined by an interior portico and is entered through a monumental main gate. Built into the back wall of the enclosure, on axis with the main gate, a large rectangular hall usually houses the principal Buddha images. The statues of Buddha and various attendant bodhisattvas and guardians typically sit arrayed along the back wall on a raised platform, some providing a special place before the central icon for the officiating priest. Worshipers line themselves up in front of the platform to perform their prayers and make their offerings.

In the courtyard, sometimes lined up along the main axis, some-times astride it, stand two separate kinds of structure. One is typically the reliquary pagoda (some temples have a pair of them), and the other is a one- (or occasionally two-) story rectangular hall, considerably smaller than the main hall to the rear, originally used for worship before an altar. Lecture halls, dining rooms, dormitories, bell towers, store houses, and other service facilities are typically arranged outside the immediate tem-ple precincts, sometimes gathered in by larger wall–enclosures that fea-ture monumental gates. In Japan a number of very important complexes cluster many subtemples around the nucleus of the principal temple buildings. There the subtemples function chiefly as residential facilities with their own refectories and group meditation halls. Though there are many similarities in the shapes and building types Buddhists have devel-oped in China, Korea, and Japan, decorative tastes in the three regions are significantly different. As a broad generalization, it is fair to suggest that whereas subdued natural tones tend to predominate in Japanese temples, Korean temples sport much more color and complex decoration; Chinese temples are somewhere in between.

Landscape and garden design are virtually indispensable features of Japanese Buddhist architecture. Meditation gardens of several varieties provide a serene ambience. Some include running water amid the vegeta-tion. Most common are those that combine carefully arranged plantings with specially chosen boulders and gravel raked in wavelike patterns. Some use only patterned gravel, which receives a new design daily under the rake of a monk assigned to conceive the work as a meditative exercise.

Some gardens serve large communal spaces where many people can enjoy them either from rooms whose screen–walls open wide or from verandas that surround the garden on two or more sides. In especially well-accoutered monastery–temples, individual monks can slide the screens of their cells open to revel in their own personal gardens. These are living, three-dimensional counterparts to the extraordinary landscape scrolls to whose development many Buddhist monk artists contributed.

60. How did Buddhist visual arts develop their iconographic themes, and how do they function in Buddhist life?

As dawn portends sunrise, so friendship with the beautiful portends wisdom's arising in the monk. So said the Buddha to his monks, according to an early text in the Pali Canon. Buddhist art, a vast monument to friendship with the beautiful, tells the story of the spiritualization of an exemplary human being. In its images of human potential, it portrays the ultimate goal of life, sought through reliance on personal resources and the Buddha's teaching or through appeal to other-power in the saving grace of the celestial Buddhas and bodhisattvas. Buddhist art depicts the gradual dehistoricization and universalization of the Buddha. Even the earliest art did not attempt to show the Buddha as he actually was. Two interpretations have arisen to explain the veiled imagery of early Buddhist art. The first is that early Buddhist art is aniconic—that out of respect for the sacred person, the oldest extant imagery leaves the Buddha out altogether using symbols to represent his presence. Like the early Christians who used a fish or a plain cross to symbolize Christ, the first Buddhist artists indicated the presence of the Buddha through symbols like a parasol, a riderless horse, an empty throne beneath a tree, or footprints on the water. Another interpretation is that the imagery was not intended to represent the Buddha himself but rather sacred places or events associated with the Buddha's life, many of which had become places of pilgrimage.

It was likely Hellenistic influence in northwest India that gave rise to the first anthropomorphic images of the Buddha. Buddhist images in turn appear to have provided a major impetus to the rise of Hindu religious arts. These elegant stone creations made no attempt to portray the Buddha as such but communicated instead an idealized vision of his enlightened being. Because he had become extinct in nirvana, it made no sense to hold on to his prenirvanic human form. A basic iconographic vocabulary included such elements as the topknot and cornrow hair, the monk's robe draped over the left shoulder, the meditative lotus posture, and various hand gestures indicating specific moments in his experience and teaching. As monasteries became more permanent and pilgrimage centers multiplied, Buddhist art could be produced on a larger scale and kept in protected settings.

Visual arts played an enormous role in Buddhism's inculturation as it moved east and southeast into Asia. At first, works that missionaries brought with them set the aesthetic standard and local artists hesitated to take liberties with the original models. But eventually regional styles developed, transforming the Buddha into a Chinese, a Korean, a Cambodian, a Japanese.

61. What are some of the other important iconographic themes in Buddhist art?

Images of the Buddha's previous lives have been especially important in Theravada tradition. Many Thai temples feature meditation murals along their inner walls, typically depicting the last 10 of the Buddha's 547 previous lives as narrated in the *Jataka* literature. Each scene represents a particular virtue as exemplified by the bodhisattva's conduct in the tale depicted. Moving from one to the next, the meditator strives to internalize the story's lesson. In addition to the murals, Southeast Asian artists have also created numerous illustrated texts of the *Jatakas* in the form of accordion-folded stiff paper manuscripts. The small portable images usually excerpt particular moments from the stories, whereas the larger format of the mural allows the artist to include multiple moments in a single frame.

All over the Buddhist world, one finds images recalling important moments in the Buddha's life. In virtually every medium, from illustrated manuscripts to nearly billboard-size posters, Buddhists use paradigmatic events to teach and inspire. Though many are inclined to think of Buddhism as purely pacific and serene, there are numerous variations on the theme of embodied holiness. Guardian figures and subsidiary deities of Hindu origin also appear prominently all over Asia, even in Theravada lands. Guardian figures are typically large, intimidating men, scowling and bristling with weaponry. Even though Buddha did not

regard Hinduism's deities as in any way essential to the Buddhist world-view, these denizens of every nook and cranny of the cosmos survive in a rich iconography. They seem to have made the transition into their east Asian forms riding the coattails of the many Buddhas and bodhisattvas, and may reflect a taste and need for an even fuller communion of inter-mediary powers.

Bodhisattvas are everywhere in Mahayana Asia, from miniature statues in home shrines to colossal mountainside stone statues that are visible for miles. The iconographic range of these images is mind-boggling, offering a variation for each of dozens of subcults. With their numerous heads that sport distinct expressions and face different direc-tions, and multiple arms that brandish special implements, the bod-hisattvas appear to be all things to all people. In some instances, sculptors have produced hundreds, even thousands, of images of the same bodhisattva in a given temple, each with a different face to indicate the compassionate being's ability to attend guardian angellike to every single individual.

62. Have there been any especially important Buddhist painters? Can one detect a distinctively Buddhist aesthetic in their work?

Some of Asia's most important painters have been Buddhist monks. One can only speculate as to the exact identity of those who cre-ated the earliest extant works, such as the cave murals at Ajanta in west-ern India from around the fifth century and through the next several centuries in Central Asia and China. Dun-huang's Caves of the Thou-sand Buddhas are generally said to be the work of professional temple painters, but it is a good bet that most, if not all, were resident monks or nuns. Not until the later medieval period, beginning around the thir-teenth century, do individual artists emerge from anonymity, revealing important Buddhist connections in detail. Perhaps the most important and famous of these were associated with Chinese Ch'an and Japanese Zen. A basic principle that influenced the early Chinese monk–artists was the conviction that one cannot express the truth in words. Only direct intuition can approach the truth, but it is possible to hint at it through allusions both verbal and visual, and the more spontaneous, the better. Because the Buddha-nature pervades all things, a painter can choose as subject any aspect of material reality. For simplicity's sake, early artists preferred monochrome ink.

Many of the greatest Chinese Buddhist scroll paintings survive in Japanese temple collections. Still-life images and landscapes are the most common themes, along with portraitlike images of Buddhas and bodhisattvas, and of important historical figures. Mu-Ch'i's thirteenth-century "Six Persimmons" is a classic Zen image of enigmatic simplicity: Five stemmed rounded forms in varying shades of gray stand in a row. Just below the line, a sixth, dark form appears either to have been crowded out by the others or to have just arrived, attempting to squeeze into the group. That's it. What is it, one might ask? Surely it symbolizes something? Six persimmons that are thoroughly themselves, in an asymmetrical composition including lots of empty space.

Buddhist landscape paintings, called "mountain–water pictures," suggest the profound influence of Daoist themes. *Yang,* the male principle, is dry and bright and mountainous; *yin,* the female, is moist, dark, and associated with the valley. Where *yang* and *yin* blend in perfect harmony, there is *ch'i,* the misty, nebulous cosmic life force or spirit. Nature dominates, with dwellings nestled unobtrusively among the crags and pines, and one or two tiny human figures meditating or going about their ordinary tasks, dwarfed by the grandeur of the scene. Chinese Buddhist painters continued to develop their art for centuries, some attracted to the monastic life precisely because it promised the kind of refuge a serious artist needs. Japan's earliest prominent Buddhist painters emerged in the fourteenth and fifteenth centuries, modeling their landscapes after Chinese works of the Sung dynasty.

My own favorite Buddhist painter, one who stands right near the top of my list of all-time great artists, is a Zen priest named Sesshu (1420–1506). He spent most of his adult life in Kyoto but traveled extensively in China, where he learned a range of painting styles. Celebrated often as the man who put a uniquely Japanese stamp on Chinese landscape art, Sesshu mastered both the more technical "northern" and the softer, more impressionistic "southern" Sung Chinese styles. With bold swift strokes in gray and black, Sesshu draws the viewer into an amazing world as irresistible as it is stark. His artistic descendants carried Sesshu's influence throughout Japan.

Calligraphy is an art closely related to Buddhist monochrome ink painting. Using the same principles of spontaneity and studied nonchalance, the calligrapher uses a brush to paint a Chinese character or two on a large rectangular piece of rice paper. In this case, the word is itself the image; its very shape is picture enough.

63. I've seen numerous statues of the Buddha in museums. How important is religious sculpture in Buddhism? Are there rules for crafting these images?

Buddhist sculpture began to grow in importance after about the second century. Usually of cypress or bronze for indoor images and stone for outdoor uses, images of the Buddha alone (Theravada) and of the many Buddhas and bodhisattvas (Mahayana) soon became a liturgical necessity. Depending on the size of the statue, sculptors might use anywhere from one to six blocks of wood, generally carving out the inside to prevent cracking. Theravada Buddhists have been especially fond of colossal images of the Buddha reclining on his right elbow as he enters parinirvana. A perennial favorite in Thailand has been a walking Buddha who smiles as he makes a teaching gesture with his right hand. But by far the most common posture in which sculptors have depicted the Buddha is the meditative lotus position, with the specific meaning of each icon indicated by a variety of hand gestures called *mudras*. Most popular among them are the meditation gesture, hands resting on lap with palms up and laid one over the other; the "earth-touching" gesture in which the right hand drapes over the right knee with the index finger pointing downward, indicating the moment at which Buddha called the earth to witness that he had overcome Mara's temptation; and the combination of protective gesture in which the right hand is turned upward and palm out, with a gesture symbolizing the granting of a request in which the left is turned downward with palm out.

Bodhisattva statues appear standing or sitting with about equal frequency. Unlike the Buddha, who never (to my knowledge) has more than one head and two arms, bodhisattvas are often depicted with multiple heads and arms.

Whatever the thematic content or specific iconography of the images—and what I have said applies also to painted images—Buddhist sculptors all over have pursued their art keenly aware of certain canons of perfect proportion and style. A kind of sacred geometry dictated the relative size of the various portions of the Buddha body, from the height

of the head and trunk, to the length of arms, hands, feet and ears, to the placement of navel and shape of the topknot. Even now, sculptors of explicitly religious icons remain faithful to ancient stipulations. Classic Buddhist sculptures are still among the most highly valued of all national treasures in many countries of Asia.

64. Does music play a significant role in Buddhist religious life?

Music has been an important part of Buddhist practice since very early in its history, with chanting of scriptural texts dating back to at least several centuries B.C.E. Over the years, a number of variations have developed. In Japan, reciters now accompany their chanting only with the hollow "clop" of a wood block to keep everyone in rhythm. Bells are also a regular liturgical implement, as are various types of gong and drum. There is an appealing simplicity to the sounds they emit, an austere invitation to focus one's thoughts. Large metal bowl-shaped gongs produce a rich, lingering-yet-fading resonance whose very decay into silence is a reminder of impermanence. Such percussion instruments are perhaps the most common in temple settings, but wind and string instruments also have an important place in various cultures. Tibetan Buddhists use a very large unvalved trumpet that produces a single baritone note sounded over and over. Played together with clanging symbols and thumping drums of various sizes, the trumpets contribute to what seems to an outsider as a cacophonous din; but to the participants, these are numinous sounds that give voice to the unseen world.

Tibetan chanting itself is a most intriguing aspect of Buddhist religious music. Years of special training allow monks of the Gelug-pa order to recite their scriptures at pitches that sound inhumanly low. But what is more astounding is that they can produce two notes by causing their vocal cords to produce an overtone or harmonic in addition to a fundamental tone. On first hearing, one is inclined to think something must be seriously wrong somewhere in the room. This initially unnerving sonority can eventually begin to have a calming effect, however, and one can arrive at a sense of its ability to evoke feelings of contact with another dimension of existence. Part of the experience involves visualizing innumerable deities of music filling the air. Only a person who has achieved authentic meditative absorption *(samadhi)* can produce this sound, the tradition teaches, and such a chanter has the power to communicate that spiritual state to one who listens with appropriate disposition. This is prayer–music in which sound and meaning are inseparable.

Solo and ensemble instruments capable of melodies and harmonies have also been useful in communicating Buddhist meanings and moods. One of the more atmospheric is the Japanese *shakuhachi,* a bamboo flute that has come to be associated with the sound of Zen. Most music composed for shakuhachi is meditative and religious in its general associations. With its soft, haunting voice, the shakuhachi is often immediately appealing across cultural boundaries. That is not true of all Buddhist instrumental music. China is perhaps the most prominent source of Buddhist ensemble music, evidently as a result of Buddhism's age-old competition with Daoism, which had a long history of instrumental ensemble music by the time Buddhism arrived. Some Chinese traditional ensembles use tenor plucked strings and high woodwinds that make thin, reedy sounds that can grate on the unattuned ear. All Buddhist ritual music, nevertheless, seeks to establish a mood conducive to prayer and meditation.

65. Have Buddhists cultivated creative forms of literature as vehicles for religious thought?

Buddhist poetry begins with Indian writers who used Sanskrit literary forms as vehicles for articulating often theoretical and complex philosophical and psychological themes. Many of these authors were monks, like the south Indian poet Shantideva (fl. ca. 700), whose poetry was largely pedagogical. Buddhists in virtually every region of Asia have developed a range of other literary forms as well, including important lyric genres whose allusions to Buddhist teachings are more subtle and indirect than those of didactic poetry. Here I will refer to only two of the many rich treasuries of Buddhist artistic literary creativity, examples from China and Japan.

One of the earliest bodies of Buddhist poetry developed in China during the T'ang dynasty (618–907). Like the other artists in traditional societies, poets need patrons to survive. Buddhism enjoyed strong support under T'ang emperors until a Daoist ruler ascended the throne in 845 and made life difficult for Buddhists. There has always been an intimate relationship between poetry and painting in China as well as elsewhere in east Asia. Important Buddhist poets, many of them monks, have also been painters and have expressed an exquisite sensitivity to nature and landscape with both pen and brush. Buddhism's teaching of a salvation from life's difficulties invited quiet reflection in mountain monasteries and temple retreats where the privilege of leisure could set creative impulse at liberty. Much Chinese Buddhist poetry, often physically attached to landscape paintings, describes the power of nature to guide seekers toward freedom from spiritual encumbrances. Works of poet–painter Wang Wei (701–761) offer some of the finest glimpses of a Chinese artistic vision of Buddhism. After his wife died, Wang opted for celibacy and converted his home to a monastery. Withdrawing from society, he pursued Ch'an meditation. Wang Wei was only one of many great Buddhist poets of China whose works, even in English translation, are quite powerful and engaging.

Perhaps the best-known literary genre associated with Buddhism is the Japanese Zen-related *haiku* ("mad phrase"). The 17 syllable (three verses, 5–7–5) poem's dry economy of form hides a powerfully evocative insight born of meditation, usually conjuring up images from nature. The haiku's brevity and conciseness makes it the literary counterpart of the spontaneously crafted Chinese character or landscape painting: Don't think about it too much, and certainly don't talk it to death. In one much used example of the form—Ah, the old pond/In jumps a frog/The liquid plop!—the poet attends to the utterly homely and obvious but so often overlooked features of ordinary life. Deceptively simple, the haiku became a quintessential Zen pedagogical device reminiscent of the koan. Intuition is the key.

66. Have dance, drama, or other performance arts been important in Buddhist religious ritual or entertainment?

As part of the larger phenomenon of ritual movement and gesture, dance plays some role in virtually every religious tradition. Its most basic forms are the nearly universal practices of procession and circumambulation, while the more elaborate vary a great deal from one cultural setting to another. Dance and gesture pick up where words fail and allow celebrants to become more fully engaged in worship. Sometimes these activities function as a protective device, banishing evil from the company of worshipers. Sometimes dance is more joyous and festive, and sometimes only ritual specialists perform, so that the dance takes on the aspect of performance rather than of participation. Although elaborate ritual movement and gesture seem less central in Buddhist tradition than, for example, in Hinduism, Buddhists have cultivated a variety of forms.

Dancing is an integral part of certain Buddhist religious rituals in the Himalaya kingdoms where Vajrayana lineages are especially influential. In Tibet, for example, a circular dance in which participants leap as they whirl is a method for imitating the divine. Dancers achieve enlightenment by realizing the unity of the divine and the individual's inner spiritual movements. Some types of dance eventually retreat from ritual prominence into religious entertainment. A type of masked dramatic performance called *gigaku* originated in China and made its way to Japan where it enjoyed the patronage of the emperor as a way of making Buddhism known more widely. Originally a procession in which masked performers parodied all manner of sinful behavior, *gigaku* survives in two forms: the popular east Asian Lion Dance and a Japanese procession in which monks visually reconstruct an image of the Buddhist spiritual cosmos by circumambulating a statue of the Buddha while wearing bodhisattva masks.

Buddhist elements are especially strong in several forms of Japanese theater. Ancient Noh plays featured Buddhist guardian divinities doing battle with demons. During medieval times, Buddhist temples housed acting companies engaged in retelling stories of the Buddha. Later theatrical forms called Kabuki and Bunraku also centered on Buddhist themes, such as that of Amida extending his saving mercy to a once-powerful person who has ended up in hell. Thailand, a region famous for its exquisite traditions of dance, also developed several varieties of narrative-symbolic enactments of Buddhist sacred story. Scenes from the Buddha's previous lives as told in the Jatakas are a prominent theme in Thai dance-theater.

The ancient Chinese, and later Japanese, "tea ceremony" is a type of performance art in that precise rules govern its practice, and the "guests" are served spiritual sustenance as well as tea. Far more than merely a stylized form of hospitality, the tea ceremony is very much in the spirit of Zen. Each detail of the tea room and its implements, and every slow, deliberate gesture of the host or hostess calls for uncluttered attentiveness. Spare display of leaves and grasses, a scroll with a single exquisitely written Chinese character, a treasured lacquer tea box, a delicate stirring whisk of bamboo, an unremarkable ceramic cup, all invite unhurried presence and appreciation, and awareness that nothing here is superfluous. Everything is only its simple, humble self, but everything is here, now, and needs no other credentials. Those few moments out of time that the tea ceremony offers are a tonic to the soul and a welcome reminder of the clarion awareness at the center of Buddhist enlightenment.

Seven:

Relationships to Other Religious Traditions

67. How would you describe Buddhism's relationship to Hinduism?

Depending on one's point of view, one could describe Buddhism's relationship to Hinduism as either rejection, reform, or reincarnation. Because I have addressed many of the individual issues in earlier questions, I will merely recall them in summary fashion here.

From the perspective of Brahmin orthodoxy, Buddhism was one of a number of heretical sectarian developments that rejected central tenets such as the caste system and the dominance of the priestly caste. Even though, strictly speaking, the Buddha did not mount a serious denial of the existence of the gods, he might as well have because he regarded them with indifference. Along with other groups that mainstream Hindu thought labeled "nay-sayers," (*nastikas,* "those who say it is not"), Buddhists rejected the authority of the Vedas. Above all, the Buddha refused to affirm the existence of an indestructible soul or ego at the center of the human personality, thereby opening a wide gap between the psychological theories of the two traditions.

From the perspective of some early Buddhists, the teaching of the Enlightened One amounted to a reform of notions that time had warped almost beyond recognition. They believed that Buddhism represented a renewed understanding of the concepts of the implications of human action (karma), of the "content" of the cosmic law (dharma), and of the nature of the rebirth (no longer reincarnation or metempsychosis, strictly speaking) and the eternal round of existence (samsara). Some scholars suggest that even the concepts of impermanence (anitya) and no-soul (anatman) represent variations on Hindu themes elaborated within the six orthodox "views" *(darshanas),* profoundly radicalized understandings admittedly, rather than out and out rejections of Hindu teaching.

Finally, some Hindu thinkers saw fit to locate Buddha theologically as an avatar of Vishnu. When it became clear that Buddhism was not likely to melt away, the enormously expansive metaphor of divine descents (avatars) provided a niche for it. A variation on an old proverb: If you can't beat 'em, make it look like they've joined you.

68.   What are some significant features of Buddhism's relationship to Jainism?

Jainism, like Buddhism, was one of the more important *nastika* Indian sects in the late sixth century B.C.E. Both registered vigorous reactions against the power of the Brahmanical priesthood and the primal authority of the Vedas. Jainism's founder, Nataputta Vardhamana (599–527 B.C.E., possibly a half-century later), was born near Vaishali, site of one of the early Buddhist councils. According to legend, Vardhamana, like Gautama, grew up amid luxury and started a family but rejected it all at age 30 (Gautama did so at 29). Opting for the strictest forms of asceticism of the sort Gautama would reject, Vardhamana associated himself with Goshala, the teacher of an ascetic order called the Ajivakas. Goshala denied not only the existence of gods but also the very possibility of improving one's lot by ethical conduct. After a falling out with Goshala, Vardhamana continued the life of a naked wanderer, enduring all manner of severity and avoiding even the slightest harm to any creature. Like Gautama, he sought insight and found it, conquering his embodiment in nirvana and earning the titles Jina, the Conqueror, and Mahavira, the Great Hero.

Jainism developed a tradition of monasticism, with monks (and nuns in one of the two main sects) vowing to refrain from injury, lying, stealing, sexual pleasure, and all attachment, a notch or two up the austerity scale from Buddhist practice generally. Lay Jains profess a dozen vows, each challenging enough but spread out over a broad array of demands that were considerably less demanding in total than the monastic requirements: no killing, even indirectly, no lying, stealing, unchastity, greed, acquisitiveness, avoidable evil; and practices of meditation, self-denial, visits to a monastery, and alms. Many Jains regard their tradition's relationship to Hinduism much the way many Buddhists regard theirs, namely, as a kind of reform movement. Unlike Buddhism, Jain teaching does not deny the existence of soul but regards soul as a veritable magnet for deleterious karma that weighs it down. A soul liberated through asceticism retains uninterrupted consciousness in its hard-won freedom.

69. What are some of the main features of Buddhism's relationship to Confucianism?

Confucius (c. 551–479 B.C.E.) and Buddha were almost exact contemporaries, but the worlds in which they lived could hardly have been more diverse. Buddhism's Chinese inculturation transformed the tradition into a reality quite different from its Indian prototype. By the time Buddhism entered China through Central Asia, Confucian tradition was well established as a kind of ethical and intellectual orthodoxy as well as political philosophy for imperial rule. One issue in particular slowed Buddhism's acceptance: Many Chinese looked askance at Buddhist monastic renunciation in general and celibacy in particular because it went against the grain of the filial piety and the centrality of family that is so prominent in Confucianism.

Early Chinese Buddhists showed great adaptability in their choice of Chinese conceptual equivalents for Sanskrit and Pali terms. But something is bound to be lost in translation, and in this instance, Confucian formality and penchant for precisely delimited human relationships was the winner. For example, Buddhism's inclusive concept of "morality and conduct" (shila) became the Confucian notion of "filial obedience and docility." In Indian Buddhism's language of social relations, husband supported wife and wife comforted husband; deferring to Confucianism, Chinese Buddhist language has husband controlling wife and wife revering husband. Terms of endearment that suggested overt expression of emotion, such as the kisses and embraces a devotee offers a bodhisattva in Sanskrit texts, vanished from Chinese Buddhism.

An already ancient Chinese method called "matching concepts" *(ko-i)* also provided a precedent for Buddhist inculturation. Teachers would pair clusters of related Buddhist notions with Confucian traditional Chinese clusters. They likened Buddhism's five lay precepts to Confucianism's five "constant virtues" (humanity, uprightness, knowledge of rites, wisdom, trust) and the five "great elements" of Buddhism (earth, air, fire, water, ether) to the "five energies" (earth, fire, water, wood, metal) of Confucian thought. The bodhisattva's career and vows were likened to the Confucian sage's control of emotions and practice of the Golden Mean. To increase Buddhism's appeal to Confucian society, teachers emphasized their tradition's stress on a filial piety that actually did the Confucian concept one better by including in its salvific embrace not only individual families and their ancestors but the whole family of humanity. The Buddha left home not to reject his father but to show gratitude to his parents by seeking the Way of Heaven *(Dao)* and enlightenment.

As Buddhism began to ramify into various new lineages of Chinese origin, some seemed to lean toward the slower, more methodical, and self-disciplined path toward enlightenment favored by Theravada tradition. Some scholars attribute this "gradualist" proclivity to the influence of Confucianism, which prescribed a long, demanding, analytical education as well as the observance of strict social hierarchy and ritual precision. Analogies of this sort are entirely relative, however, and one has to invoke them with due caution, because even the schools of Buddhism most inclined to a gradual approach were still on a very fast track by contrast to the Confucian approach. Meanwhile, Buddhism was changing the way Confucians understood their own tradition. As a result, when neo-Confucian thinkers spurred a revival during the Sung dynasty (eleventh to thirteenth century), they reinterpreted the terms of the Confucian Classics with reference to the prevailing Buddhist intellectual climate.

70. What about Buddhism's relationship with the Chinese indigenous tradition called Daoism?

Confucianism was a major component in Buddhist inculturation, but it faced the sometimes stiff competition of Daoism, both in the royal patronage sweepstakes and in the tug-of-war over influence on the changing shape of Buddhism. When Buddhism came to China, Daoist thought was gaining strength in relation to Confucianism. Philosophical Daoism, traditionally traced to Lao Tzu and Chuang Tzu, perhaps fourth and third centuries B.C.E., experienced something of a revival from around 200 to 400 C.E. Around 200, China witnessed what some scholars consider to be the beginnings of Daoism as a distinct religious tradition. An expanding Daoist pantheon made it relatively natural for many Chinese to respond hospitably to the new deity called Buddha and even to consider Buddhism a Daoist sect. Daoists found Buddhism's unusual recipes for attaining salvation and immortality, and for engaging the myriad supernatural forces, especially appealing.

As early as the mid-second century C.E. the notion arose that Lao-tzu, traditionally believed to have vanished mysteriously, became a Buddha and embarked on a missionary journey to convert the world to Daoism. Daoism's central concept of "the Way" seemed a natural counterpart for either dharma or *bodhi* (enlightenment). Buddhism's term for enlightened person, arhat, became the Daoist "immortal" *(chen-jen),* and nirvana became the classic and paradoxical Daoist notion of "noneffort" *(wu-wei).* Under Buddhist influence, Daoists organized a scriptural canon in three parts in imitation of the Buddhist Tripitaka, began to structure their religious doctrine formally, and developd an iconography of their sacred personalities. Some scholars suggest that Daoism became an unwitting vehicle for the spread of Buddhist teachings.

If the relative "gradualism" of Chinese Pure Land and Tendai lineages suggests the influence of Confucianism, the "subitism" of Chen Yen and Ch'an is arguably Daoism's dowry in this marriage of traditions. Daoism advocated a more organic, less linearly rational quest for an elusive treasure whose very unexpectedness was a measure of its authenticity. In addition, Ch'an use of meditative techniques mirror the Daoist affinity with nature as the perfect stimulus to reflection. Monasticism was another important link between Daoism and Buddhism, especially the two branches of Ch'an, as was the shared phenomenon of an ordained clergy, a feature absent in Confucianism.

During the fifth and sixth centuries, Buddhism experienced the beginnings of a kind of liberation movement that sought to wean it of the dependence on Daoist language that resulted from early attempts at translation. Gradually, Buddhist scholars found ways to disentangle major doctrines such as emptiness (shunyata) from Daoist associations by refining their language. But popular Buddhism continued to move toward syncretism, canonizing figures from the Daoist pantheon by conferring upon them attributes and powers formerly associated with Buddhas and bodhisattvas. Around the eleventh century, for example, Daoism's deity of war, Kuan Ti, became the "Buddha who protects the kingdom." Exchanging in the other direction, Buddhism's various afterworlds melded with popular Daoist eschatology. An important result of this two-way traffic in religious ideas and imagery has been that contemporary Chinese popular religion is a virtually homogenized blend of Daoism and Buddhism.

71. How did Buddhism interact with Shinto, Japan's indigenous tradition? Was the process of inculturation in Japan anything like "dialogue"?

Shinto is the most ancient of Japan's religious traditions. Because it had no historical founding figure, it is impossible to date the origins of Shinto, but distinctive traces of its myth and ritual appear from as early as the third century B.C.E. As is often the case in the history of religious traditions, the eternal "Way of the Kami" (*kami-no michi* in Japanese, *kami* referring to "high, numinous beings") did not acquire the name by which it is now most commonly known until it became necessary to distinguish it from a rival tradition. When the "Way of the Buddha" *(butsu-do)* came to Japan in the sixth century, the indigenous "Way of the Kami" got its new name, *Shin-to* (from the Chinese *shen-dao,* "way of the gods"). Buddhism's historic interaction with Shinto has had a profound impact on both traditions since the very beginning.

During its early Japanese (mid-sixth through eighth) centuries, Buddhism enjoyed a good deal of imperial support, while the number of Shinto shrines grew to more than 3,000 with about one-fourth of them under direct government sponsorship. The Kasuga Taisha in Nara, founded by the powerful Fujiwara family, was the most important Shinto establishment, and it was at Nara that the earliest major "theological dialogue" occurred. During a smallpox epidemic in 735, the emperor commissioned at Nara the 48-feet-tall seated Daibutsu ("great Buddha"), one of the world's largest cast-bronze statues, that is now housed in Todaiji ("eastern great temple") in the world's largest all-wooden building. The emperor then sent a Buddhist patriarch as his emissary to the Shinto shrine of Ise, center of worship of the sun goddess, to beg the favor of Amaterasu. After the patriarch reported a favorable response, the emperor is said to have dreamt that Amaterasu identified herself with Vairochana, the central figure among the five transcendent Buddhas. This accommodation was of enormous significance because it associated the chief Shinto deity with the Great Buddha of Nara, Vairochana ("who is like the sun"). Fifteen years later, a symbol of the Shinto deity of war, Hachiman, was brought to Todaiji to pay respect to Vairochana, along with funds for the completion of Todaiji. In a gesture indicating that the Kami themselves would stand guard over Buddha's teachings, Hachiman (now considered a bodhisattva) remained at Todaiji in a special shrine.

During the next several centuries, a number of Buddhist teachers proclaimed that various Shinto deities were actually Buddhas and bodhisattvas in disguise and that Buddhism reveals the inner nature of Shinto. During the thirteenth and fourteenth centuries, Buddhism became part of an amalgam called the warrior code (bushido) of the shōgun's ("throne field marshal") samurai, blending a calm discipline with Shinto patriotism. As the shōgunate waxed during the fifteenth and sixteenth centuries, so did Shinto's symbolic importance as the "official" imperial tradition. By the early 1600s, a movement to restore Shinto to its original purity began to reverse historic trends, reestablishing the kamis' ancient hegemony. Turning the tables, the new teaching held that the Buddhas were local manifestations of the universal kami and that the emperor was a direct descendant of the Sun goddess. Today, thousands of Japanese Buddhist temples have a small Shinto shrine somewhere on their grounds. Although Shinto shrines do not return the favor, the deer roaming the grounds of Kasuga Taisha are a clear reminder of the Deer Park where the Buddha preached his first sermon.

72. Did the Second Vatican Council make any statements about the Catholic Church's official view of Buddhism?

In *Nostra Aetate* ("In our times…"), the "Declaration on the Relationship of the Church to Non-Christian Religions," Vatican II laid out an overview of interreligious relations. Two key statements provide the larger context within which to interpret more specific references to individual traditions. First, the Catholic Church does not reject anything "true and holy" in other faiths. Second, the church exhorts its members to communicate and work with members of other faiths to promote both "the spiritual and moral goods" that their traditions teach and the "values in their society and culture." Both statements are very constructive and allow a great deal of latitude. But just how are Catholics to interpret more precisely the operative expressions *true and holy* and *spiritual and moral goods and values?*

Vatican II pays particular attention to several major faith traditions by name, Judaism and Islam in greatest detail, with briefer but still very telling references to both Hinduism and Buddhism. Noting that the various faith traditions offer ways to address the "restless searchings of the human heart," the document characterizes the Buddhist assessment of the fundamental human predicament. Mention of "the radical insufficiency of this shifting world" recalls how the experience of impermanence led the Buddha to the Four Noble Truths and to his analysis of the radical interdependence of all things in the "wheel of conditioned origination." As for Buddhism's solution to the predicament, the council acknowledges its teaching of a path that can instill genuine confidence and devotion. Spiritual seekers can travel either alone (self-power) or with assistance (other-power), arriving at either complete freedom or supreme enlightenment. If lack of greater detail in the Vatican II statement seems a bit surprising or disappointing at first, it will help to keep in mind that *Nostra Aetate* was intended as an initial affirmation of the importance of dialogue and of positive regard for other traditions.

73. What are some of the major differences between Buddhist and Christian doctrinal systems?

Salvation is an important theme in all Christian denominations and in several Buddhist lineages, especially Pure Land with its emphasis on "other-power." But a major difference is that whereas Christianity's saving God has ultimate power over all things, the Buddhas and bodhisattvas do not generally step in to control the law of karma but only help the believer plant seeds of good karma. Even so, complete surrender to Amida can effect total purification by divine power. Still, the mediator in Buddhism remains a symbol of the Absolute, whereas for Christians Christ is the Absolute. Japan's True Pure Land school teaches a doctrine of salvation purely by faith, a faith at which one can arrive only through the practice of virtue. Most problematic of all for Buddhists is the Christian teaching of salvation through the cross. To put it mildly, we have here, as St. Paul suggested, a stumbling block.

Concepts of ultimate reality are an area of major divergence between Christianity and Buddhism. The God of Christian belief is a transcendent being who has chosen to become immanent through an incarnation in Jesus, both human teacher and divine power. Buddhism begins with human experience as understood and explained by Buddha the teacher, whom the Mahayana schools gradually elevated to the functional status of a divinity, but a divinity who in any case merely symbolizes the goal of human existence, nirvana. For Christians, absolute reality is personal; for Buddhists, it is transpersonal or beyond personality. In the Mahayana doctrine of the

Three Bodies *(trikaya)* of the Buddha some see a distant analogy to the Christian Trinity, arguing that both doctrines provide a systematic mechanism for integrating transcendence and immanence.

There is a wide gap also between the respective notions of soul. Christians believe in an immortal, indestructible spiritual essence that is closely identified with human individuality. Classical Buddhist tradition refuses to acknowledge the existence of any such permanent core that functions as an ego or focus of personality. Some scholars have suggested a possible connection, even so, in Christ's self-emptying (kenosis) and the Christian ideal of self-denial, but the two traditions are radically divergent in this respect: in Buddhist thought, nothing important depends on the existence of individual soul; in Christian thought, immortality of soul is a theological hot spot.

Buddhist teaching does not rest on a divine revelation as Christianity does. Buddha offered to point the way, Jesus proclaimed that he is the way. Truths that according to Buddhist tradition each individual must seek and discover, Christian tradition identifies as gifts freely bestowed from above.

74. What are some areas of potentially fruitful dialogue between Buddhists and Christians? Why is this important now?

Some people might wonder why Christians should even bother talking to Buddhists if the differences in beliefs are so enormous and fundamental. Others are willing to entertain thoughts of dialogue only if they believe the two sides are already close enough that the other side might eventually be persuaded to change. That, of course, is not dialogue at all, but a not-so-subtle form of manipulation. I believe that dialogue between Christians and Buddhists is of high importance precisely because of their striking differences. Perhaps the greatest benefit of dialogue is its potential for stimulating both sides to reflect more deeply on what they believe and why. I can think of no tradition more capable of encouraging Christians to serious consideration of their own convictions than Buddhism.

Buddhists and Christians share a number of important issues of general concern. Questions of theological anthropology that can illuminate our common understandings about the nature and inherent value of the human person, and of moral responsibility and social obligation, are a good starting point. At the heart of such questions are themes that can engage us profoundly on both sides. We need to explore, for example, ways in which Buddhist interpretations of compassion *(karuna)* and Christian understandings of love *(agape)* might illuminate one another. Buddhism's dead aim at problems of human suffering and ways to freedom from suffering can further stimulate Christian reflection such as various proponents of Liberation Theology have begun. Buddhism's sense of global sister- and brotherhood and of humanity's continuity with all sentient beings makes a natural point of contact with ancient Christian themes such as Francis of Assisi's spirituality of nature, and Christianity's deeply rooted convictions about how a search for justice might play out globally is a natural link to the Buddhist concept of cosmic harmony.

75. What was Thomas Merton's connection with Buddhism?

Thomas Merton (1915–1968) was a monk of the Cistercian Order who spent much of his life in the abbey at Gethsemani, Kentucky. In his later years, this convert to Catholicism became intensely interested in Asian spiritual traditions, both Hindu and Buddhist. Of the traditions he studied, he found Chinese Zen Buddhism the most appealing, and he published several pieces on Zen's distinctive approach to spiritual experience. He was especially attracted to Zen's attack on formalism, myth, and conventional religiosity. He struggled with the paradox that although Zen talks the talk of a thoroughgoing iconoclasm, its temples are nevertheless gilded havens of iconography and ritual.

Of all Buddhist beliefs, the emphasis on the compassion fully realized in the bodhisattva attracted Merton more than any other. He also seemed intrigued by Buddhism's repudiation of doctrine as the final word. Though that feature locates Buddhism at virtually the opposite end of the truth spectrum from Catholicism, Merton evidently found it a bracing slap of intellectual honesty that brought back to him the experiential core of his own faith: The truth of Christianity is not embalmed in elegant formulae but alive in a person who unites all things. Merton searched for a way to discover genuinely comparable elements in the two traditions. Does one compare ritual, prayer, ethics, mysticism? And how broad a swath does one cut in the traditions, including how many varieties and from how many cultural settings? Perhaps, he thought, one should compare one Christian figure with one Buddhist, but the question remained as to whether and how well any single figure could be taken to represent a whole tradition. Attracted as he was to mysticism in various traditions, Merton stopped well short of identifying mystical experience as a common ground on which all differences evaporate and all taste the same reality. Perhaps there is common ground where Christianity speaks of taking on the "mind of Christ" and Buddhism "the Buddha mind."

In the final analysis, Merton asked, Is Zen practice a common ground for both traditions? On a nondoctrinal level, perhaps, as a Christian might find yogic exercise spiritually helpful without converting to Hinduism. In Merton's own experience, the Zen alarm clock rang, and he woke up a Christian. Through his expanding network of monastic connections, Merton became one of Roman Catholicism's most visible and credible proponents of interreligious dialogue. He died in Bangkok while attending an intermonastic congress.

76. Is the phenomenon of monasticism a significant link between Christianity and Buddhism?

Monasticism may be the single most important organizational bridge between the two traditions. Buddhist monasticism is possibly the oldest continuously functioning institution anywhere, and Catholic monasticism is second only to the papacy for longevity in Christian history. A dozen years ago, I attended a conference on prayer, one of a series sponsored by the Naropa Institute, a Tibetan Buddhist foundation in Boulder, Colorado. All of the major Christian presenters were members of monastic orders. Perhaps the topic made monastic involvement especially appropriate, but it is clear, even so, that monks and nuns have been responsible for a great deal of fruitful Buddhist–Christian dialogue in our time.

Thomas Merton was neither the first nor the last influential Christian monk to engage in dialogue with his Buddhist counterparts. A Monastic Interreligious Dialogue group made up of members of various Catholic monastic orders organizes exchanges in which monks and nuns from both traditions spend time in each others' communities. In July 1996, Gethsemani Abbey hosted a conference of some 50 representatives to discuss a series of problematic doctrinal issues. Points of note-worthy concordance centered around practices of prayer and the medita-tive reading or recitation of scripture. At the end of the meeting, all participants gathered around the grave of Thomas Merton, who had been so committed to monastic dialogue 30 years earlier.

Eight:

Women and Family

77. Can women achieve enlightenment and salvation? Can they become Buddhas?

To understand how Buddhist tradition has treated the spiritual status of women, it is important to see first how the Buddha's teaching represented a significant change from the dominant attitudes of the Indian culture of his day. Brahmanical Hinduism in the Buddha's India generally relegated women to a very low rung on the ladder of spiritual value. With virtually no prospect of liberation on her own, a woman's only chance of improving her lot over the long haul of many lifetimes was to marry and benefit from her husband's higher status. Buddhist teaching, along with its repudiation of caste, addressed this issue very early on: Women were not mere chattel, could contribute to society apart from raising children, and were capable of spiritual progress on their own. This very dramatic shift of attitude acknowledged human value in women of every age, from young girls to older widows. From the perspective of contemporary concern for gender-inclusive language, early Buddhist texts are striking in that they typically speak of both women and men, mother and father, in that order, and that mention of parents replaces a more pervasive Hindu concern for fathers. In general, therefore, Indian women enjoyed greater equality with men in early Buddhist tradition than they had previously. Major discrepancies, nevertheless, remained to be overcome.

Evidence on the spiritual status of Buddhist women varies somewhat with time and place. From very early times, Buddhist sources state quite directly that women need first to be reborn as men before they can advance toward enlightenment and beyond. Where, you may ask, is the advance here? Though it may seem cold comfort from our perspective, the idea that a woman could improve her lot without the aid of a man was a very significant change, even if women still had to pass through a male lifetime before proceeding further. A larger problem, however, is the persistence in Buddhist sources of the pervasive Indian belief that women are uncontrollably seductive. Whereas Hindu myth found a way to blend sexual energy with the best in maternal instincts in more than

127

one goddess, Buddhist tradition continued to regard female sexuality as almost entirely negative. Among the lists of vows associated with some of the great bodhisattvas, one invariably finds a promise to come to the aid of women, to relieve them of their alleged susceptibility to distraction by temptations of the flesh and of the burden of pregnancy and childbirth. Women thus vexed need only to hear the name of the bodhisattva Mañjushri to be delivered from the sufferings of their gender. It is safe to suggest that women did not formulate these vows.

On the other hand, some Mahayana texts in particular offer hints that the question of woman's ability to achieve enlightenment and even become a Buddha was a live issue in certain circles. The Lotus Sutra, for example, tells of how a very virtuous princess of the Nagas (serpentlike mythical creatures) offered the jewel on her forehead, perhaps a token of her sexuality, and the Buddha received it without hesitation. In spite of the fact that she was then instantly transformed into a male, the important point is that she possessed as a woman all the virtues required for Buddhahood. According to Nichiren's interpretation of the Lotus Sutra as the central text of his True Pure Land school, a woman could achieve Buddhahood. A Chinese text also speaks of the enlightenment of a laywoman while still a woman.

Buddhist rejection of caste distinction clearly did not run to its logical conclusion with respect to women. Persistence of the gender gap throughout Buddhist history is, however, less a function of Buddhist teaching itself than of the stubbornly patriarchal societies in which it took root. The social ferment occurring all over the world in our time will inevitably bring further change to the status of women who call themselves Buddhists.

78. What role have nuns played in Buddhist life? Are there significant differences in monastic rules for monks and for nuns?

When the Buddha established the monastic order of the *sangha,* he set up parallel institutions for men and women. One story has it that he resisted accepting women until one of his aunts persuaded him to do so. Even then, however, the Buddha apparently formulated additional disciplinary regulations for the female side of the order. Women needed to defer to men, even to junior monks. Even so, it is clear that women from nearly every age and social class voluntarily joined the order. It is also clear that in some contexts women pursued their Buddhist training on an equal footing with their male colleagues. In Hindu society, women could scarcely abide within earshot of chanted scripture. Buddhist women could study and recite the sacred texts, though there remained a strong suspicion that women were more naturally inclined to distraction than men and thus could not be expected to interiorize the teaching as profoundly.

Evidence of women rising to positions of authority within the sangha is extremely sparse. A Vietnamese Zen *(Thien)* lineage introduced to southeast Asia in 580 by an Indian teacher named Vinitaruci includes a nun named Dieu-nhan (d. 1115) as its seventeenth patriarch and perhaps the only woman to reach such a rank in Buddhist history. Nowadays several of the ordination lineages, in Tibet and Japan for example, required for women to achieve official and full membership in the sangha have been irreparably broken as a result of lapses in transmission from teacher to students. Even in those instances, however, there are groups of women who call themselves nuns. Perhaps the most numerous groups of Buddhist nuns are those of major Chinese lineages, some of which have established branch temples in America.

79. You mentioned at one point that Buddhist monks are ordained. Is there a ceremony like that for women who become nuns? Does it have anything like the significance it has in some Christian traditions?

Buddhist ordination to the monastic sangha, sometimes called "initiation" *(upasampada,* "taking up the same path"), involves two phases for both men and women. After a two-year novitiate, if superiors (senior nuns) and members of the chapter judge a candidate ready for full incorporation into the order, she is admitted to the higher initiation. The novice comes to the appointed place and asks three times for initiation. Part of the ceremony recorded in the Pali texts has the probationer answering 26 questions as to her suitability for ordination as a full-fledged mendicant nun. Questions covered 24 matters that might disqualify a candidate, including 11 gynecological problems and 5 diseases.

After the first 16 questions about her health, the novice had to answer an additional 10 questions, several very telling about the place of women in early Buddhist society. She was asked whether she was: a human being (to keep out beings who might take human form), a female (to rule out eunuchs), a free woman (to weed out slaves), debt free, a servant of the king (that is, exempt from military duty and therefore not obliged to kill), in possession of parents' permission (or, if married, her husband's), at least 20 years old (at or beyond marriageable age), and equipped with a robe and begging bowl. Finally the candidate was asked her name and the name of her sponsor within the order.

If the novice answered all well and was judged of suitable character and agreeable temperament, and if she was not pregnant or nursing, one of the nuns would make three proposals that they accept the candidate. Then, however, the woman would undergo the same questioning from her male counterparts, a situation that sometimes gave rise to considerable embarrassment for both men and women. Ordinarily, the scrutiny before the monks was a formality that rubber-stamped the approval of the nuns' chapter, but the monks had the authority to reverse a decision made by the women. The monks then commissioned the nuns to teach their new member the basic disciplines and reminded the new member that hers would be a life in community because it was not safe for a woman to live as a solitary mendicant. Ordained Buddhist men are often called priests, and they are able to perform a variety of religious rituals for the laity. Nuns, not generally referred to as priestesses, also perform certain rituals and lead in prayer, depending on circumstances and whether they are attached to an institution over which monks have primary authority.

80. I've heard the sacred figure named Kwan Yin in China referred to as "the Goddess of Mercy." Could you explain that?

Bodhisattva gender raises some very interesting questions for students of Buddhism. Strictly speaking, women do not become bodhisattvas or Buddhas as women. There are, however, a number of bodhisattvas whose mythic histories give evidence of considerable gender bending. China's Kwan Yin and Japan's counterpart Kannon represent one of the most intriguing examples of mythic adaptability in the history of religion. Like all the bodhisattvas, the Indian Buddhist Avalokiteshvara ("Lord who looks down") began as a male figure. One of his earliest important associations was as attendant to Vairochana Buddha presiding over the northwest, as one of four bodhisattvas cosmically arrayed with the four directional Buddhas. In subsequent developments in China and Japan, Avalokiteshvara became the bodhisattva associated with water, one of the four elements. The more popular he became as an intermediary between ordinary humans and the transcendent Buddha-nature, the more he became associated with the very embodiment of compassion, and the more he became she.

In China and Japan, statues of Kwan Yin and Kannon are perhaps more numerous than any image other than that of the meditating Buddha. Sculpted renderings seem ambivalent as to this bodhisattva's gender because although the face is usually quite feminine, the torso is clearly not. Popular lore says that some beings are powerful enough to change their gender long enough to secure salvation. Of the 33 "official" manifestations of Kannon, roughly half are either unambiguously or predominantly feminine in appearance and attributes, and nearly all have strikingly feminine countenances. Some Buddhists worship Kannon as a "great mother," but perhaps the most popular of the dozens of forms are the Japanese "Eleven-headed" and "Thousand Armed" Kannons. They bear certain attributes of the Hindu goddess Uma, consort of Shiva. The multiplicity of heads and limbs, sometimes multiplied still more dramatically by gathering hundreds of life-size images with individualized facial features in a single temple room, communicates this bodhisattva's absolute attentiveness to each being's every need in all realms.

Juntei ("The Pure") Kannon is one of the unambiguously feminine forms, with attributes possibly derived in part from another of Shiva's consorts, Durga. Called "Mother of the Buddhas," she represents fertility for some devotees and performs much the same role as a bodhisattva named Jizo in relation to children and childbirth (see Question 85). Images of her nursing a child may have been devised by Japanese Christians seeking comfort in reminders of the Virgin Mary during times of persecution in the seventeenth and eighteenth centuries. Finally, a group of 21 bodhisattvas called the Taras are often identified as female consorts or *shaktis* of the male Avalokiteshvara. The original two Taras are said to have materialized from rays of light emitted from their male counterpart's two eyes. They are especially important in Tibetan Buddhism.

81. Are there other "goddesses" in Buddhist belief?

Under the residual influence of Hindu mythology, several female figures of divine status have found places in Mahayana belief and ritual. The Hindu Sarasvati, patroness of poetry and music and consort of Brahma, made her way into Buddhist tradition as the sister of Yama, lord of Hell. Her 12 or more sons are associated with the arts as well. Her rank in the hierarchy varies from region to region, and sometimes she is reduced to the position of acolyte to the bodhisattva Kannon; but more often she has her own retinue attending her. Marici is another of the historically important goddesses, originating in Hinduism as the chief male storm demon. Her Buddhist transformation not only changes her gender (in most manifestations at least) but raises her considerably in the divine hierarchy. Medieval Japanese Buddhists found in her a powerful patroness of warriors, but her image has appeared most often in elaborate mandalas and paintings associated with small esoteric sects.

There are in addition a number of minor goddesses and deities who appear primarily in groups. Shri, a consort of Vishnu in Hindu myth, migrated to Buddhism as a patroness of good fortune and beauty, grouped among the seven goddesses of happiness in Japan. Most interestingly she is the special protector of the Dalai Lama's Tibetan lineage, the Gelug-pa. With the goddess groups, one encounters a fair amount of syncretism with the indigenous traditions, such as Tibetan shamanism and Japanese Shinto. One of the Dakinis, who were mostly associated with esoteric Tibetan Buddhism, became linked with Shinto by association with the fox–messenger Inari. Feminine deities called *shaktis,* female energy associated with male figures, are typically five in number and are paired with the Buddhas of the center and four cardinal directions. A similar group called the Five Rakshas function as protectors against all manner of disease and misfortune.

For a tradition that officially discounts the role of deities, Buddhist lore is virtually bursting with colorful and potent female personages. In addition, local tradition in nearly every Buddhist land has amalgamated figures of ancient folk beliefs with features from Buddhist lore to create unique powers often worshiped by very small populations. This dual phenomenon is a tribute both to the powerful imaginative appeal of the Hindu mythology from which many of them derive and to the ability of local and regional traditions to mold Buddhism to fit specific cultic needs.

82. I remember hearing in a Bible study course years ago that the figure of Wisdom in the Hebrew scripture was feminine. Are there any parallels in Buddhism?

A bodhisattva called Prajñaparamita, "Wisdom Going-beyond," (the second part of the name is sometimes translated "perfection") is one of the consistently feminine beings in the Buddhist pantheon. Buddhist imagery of Feminine Wisdom is strikingly similar to that of Hebrew wisdom texts, such as the Book of Proverbs, chapter 8. There the author describes how Wisdom calls out as she stands at the crossroads and on hilltops, inviting all to share in her enlightenment. In the apocryphal Book of Wisdom, Solomon describes how he sought Wisdom as a bride. Buddhist sources extol Lady Wisdom as radiant refuge, immaculate and omniscient, the nurturing protector of the vulnerable. Buddhist tradition also takes the theme considerably further than the Hebrew.

In some parts of Asia, Lady Wisdom takes the form of the bodhisattva Avalokiteshvara's female aspect. Some scholarly accounts refer to her as a goddess, but she wears the royal garb of a bodhisattva. She appears in various bodily manifestations, ordinarily with the usual number of limbs but occasionally with 11 heads and multiple arms. Texts describe her as lovely and holy, guardian of minds whose very name is a magical incantation. According to at least one school of thought, Prajña-paramita is the "Mother of all the Buddhas" and the equivalent of the female counterpart of the Adi Buddha or Buddha-nature. But she is also a virgin, untouched, a metaphor that heightens the desirability of Wisdom. She may have been the first truly independent Buddhist divinity who was beholden to no male deity for her existence.

83. Buddhist iconography features some fearsome-looking male figures. Are there similarly fearsome females?

Some of the female spiritual figures appear in a "terrible" as well as a more approachable form, but they are not nearly as prominent in Buddhism as they are in Hinduism. A female deity of the dawn from Brahmin mythology called Marici plays a guardian role and sometimes appears armed with a blade and a skull-adorned staff and dancing triumphantly over a corpse. In medieval times, Japanese warriors called on her for protection in battle. Cundi, known in Japan as Juntei Kannon, is a feminine form of Avalokiteshvara who is sometimes associated with Marici and occasionally depicted with terrifying features.

Tibetan iconography also features a number of formidable feminine personages. Kaladevi is one of eight "dharma protectors" usually depicted as embodiments of unkempt ferocity, wearing necklaces of skulls and engulfed in flame. She is the defender of Tantric sects who throws dice to set human destinies and wears a cobra as an earring and the skin of a flayed demon as an evening gown. Accompanied by fierce gods of the four seasons who guard her with single-minded devotion, Kaladevi is not one to cross. Sometimes a pair of female acolytes, every bit as businesslike as Kaladevi's male bodyguards, stand by her side. Tradition assigns her the special task of protecting the Dalai Lama.

Some of the various Taras also appear in frightening forms. The Yellow Tara, called the "frowning goddess," came into being when Avalokiteshvara scowled in displeasure. The Blue Tara, wrathful adjutant to the typically more beneficent Green Tara, stomps on cadavers and flails her weapons about with her 24 arms. Red Tara is usually of peaceful visage, but is known to wield a dangerous bow and lasso against demons. The important thing to keep in mind about all of these horrific metamorphoses is that they represent a threat only to forces of evil.

84. The Buddha and other famous teachers have stood as role models of a sort for young Buddhist men; are there similar religious role models for young women?

Buddhist religious literature is filled with stories of exemplary women, and some of them have been important models over the centuries and in various regions. That is not to say that a Buddhist woman today would find them particularly appealing, but there have of course been outstanding individuals among Buddhist women in recent times to whom many young people look for inspiration. Role models for Buddhist women must have two prominent characteristics, namely, the wisdom to attain salvation for themselves and the compassion that moves them to share that saving wisdom with others. The prospect of having to renounce one's gender in order to achieve salvation can scarcely bolster a young woman's self-esteem, but in a culture that simply sees no alternative, the image of a woman clever enough to achieve salvation while surrendering as little of herself as possible (such as the Naga Princess mentioned earlier) could very well provide a useful model. There are, however, a few suggestions in several scriptures that women might achieve high spiritual estate without compromising their gender or sexuality. A pivotal text, called *The Education of Vimalakirti (Vimalakirtinirdesha Sutra),* offers a fascinating perspective on the search for a lay spirituality that included women as equals to men. It elaborates the principle of a "nondual dharma" in which there are no discriminatory barriers among living beings and in which no living being can be definitively categorized or "conditioned" by false distinctions like male and female. In one very droll scene, a goddess wins an argument with a famous monk about her suitability for *bodhisattva*-hood without giving an inch on the question of changing her gender. The *Diamond Sutra* likewise suggests some ambiguity on the question of whether one has to be male to become a Buddha, evidently hinting at androgyny or, more precisely, asexuality.

Another unusual text features a woman who while not a goddess is nevertheless a queen and exemplifies the ability to bridge the gender gap. Queen Shrimala, said to have had the "lion's roar" generally associated with a Buddha, is the central figure in a text that describes her as a laywoman of lofty spiritual rank, a seventh- or eighth-stage bodhisattva according to some commentaries. So effective is her teaching of the dharma that all females of more than seven years of age convert immediately, followed by Shrimala's husband and all the males over seven. She embodies the doctrine of the "Buddha-womb" (*Tathagata-garbha,* also called Buddha-nature), the idea that salvation is available to all beings. Women of India, China and Japan in ancient times found her story an especially consoling example of a woman who ruled as an equal with her kingly husband.

A special case in Buddhism, as in several other traditions, is the mother of the founding figure. Buddha's mother, Maya, represents the ideal of motherhood for some segments of tradition. Like the mothers of all Buddhas and bodhisattvas, she gave birth to her son through the marvel of asexual conception and died seven days after the child's birth. Maya functions as something of a distant role model, but one who exemplifies the highest chastity as well as authority, beauty, and womanly perfection. Naturally much of her stature derives from that of her offspring, but then she would not have been so honored had it not been for her inherent excellence.

85. On a visit to Japan, we saw several temples where people had gathered hundreds of small statues with little red knit caps and children's pinwheels. What is that about?

You saw one of the more touching ritual symbols distinctive of Japanese Buddhism. A bodhisattva named Jizo (commonly referred to reverently as O-Jizo-sama) first entered the Buddhist pantheon as the Indian bodhisattva Kshitigarbha, whose name means "womb of the earth." He began his life, mythically speaking, as a young Brahmin caste Indian girl who, upon learning of the punishment her own mother was undergoing in hell, made a vow to keep all sentient beings from her mother's fate. She was eventually transformed into a bodhisattva whose name remained quite feminine but who is almost always depicted as a male. Occasionally, however, under the name Koyasu Jizo, this bodhisattva is a clearly female patron of children and giver of easy birth and fertility. Sometimes Kshitigarbha appears surrounded by the 10 kings of hell or standing in images of the 6 lands into which human beings can be reborn.

Originally an "earth mother," this bodhisattva became a kindly uncle of sorts, very approachable and much beloved. Dressed in monk's garb and carrying a pilgrim's staff, Jizo is the patron of travelers, of the dead, and of children. It has become a custom in Japan for women who have undergone abortions to purchase a small statue of Jizo and bring it to a temple, either in a special room or outside in the cemetery, as an expiatory offering. Women buy or knit tiny caps and bibs with which to clothe the statues, and some place a colorful toy with it as well. Many temples have gathered large numbers of these offerings, often referred to as "Jizo's 1000 Bodies" (*sentai jizo*). In Kamakura, for example, the Kannon Hasedera temple has become a favorite site for the ritual offerings, gathering what appear to be thousands of Jizo images, row after somber row. The unsophisticated little cemetery images are very rough icons, often scarcely more than a loaf of stone with a face. But the temple images of Jizo are much more refined. On the staff in his right hand are six rings, a symbol of his attendance upon all who need him in each of the six realms of existence. In his left he carries a wish-fulfilling gem.

86. Is "holy-family imagery" important in Buddhist piety as it is, say, in Christian and Hindu traditions?

Apart from the prominence of Buddha's mother in scripture and popular lore, Buddhist tradition does not feature the Buddha's family as a focus of devotion. There are, however, other interesting, if distant, analogies to the Christian "holy family." As happens in so many major mythological systems, Mahayana Buddhist schools have their narratives of the celestial beings, complete with family trees and heavenly pedigrees. The most unusual family image I have come across is one in which Shakyamuni Buddha is the father; Amitabha, a male Buddha and lord of the Pure Land, is the mother; and their two sons are the bodhisattva Mahasthamaprapta and another bodhisattva often associated with motherhood, Kwan Yin. Buddhist myth appropriated a great number of Hindu characters and in the process constructed whole new networks of family relations to legitimate the divine personages central to each sect. The most important familial relationship is that of consort, as in the case of several of the female deities I have already mentioned.

In Tantric spirituality, male and female principles are often paired in "father-mother" (*yab-yum*) dyads which some scholars interpret as images of androgyny rather than of sexual union as such. Common themes in the iconography of Tibet, in particular, include images of a many-armed male in a vigorous sexual embrace with his female partner. This is a couple that produce no offspring, because the nature of the relationship is not procreative but purely unitive. Children are not a prominent feature in Buddhist mythic families, except as acolytes to the main figures. There are a number of sibling relationships, but in general they play relatively minor roles in Buddhist mythological imagery.

87. Are there distinctive Buddhist rituals and views around marriage? What about divorce?

As with so many other beliefs and practices, those associated with marriage vary a great deal from one culture to another. But because Buddhist tradition generally regards marriage as a civil matter, it is not terribly difficult to separate "Buddhist" elements from local custom. The practice of arranged marriage, for example, in which the prospective spouses have little or no prior contact, is largely cultural. Ancient Buddhist tradition suggests that young women generally should marry between the ages of 16 and 20. Monogamy has been the dominant Buddhist practice since the very early days, but it is not necessarily distinctive of Buddhism as such, and there are prominent examples in history and literature of polygyny among the powerful and wealthy. As for the actual wedding ceremony, common practice in Thailand, an almost exclusively Theravada region, provides a useful example.

Many young Thai men from traditional families still spend a period of three months or more in the monastic sangha before preparing for marriage. After his family has secured the agreement of a young woman's family to give their daughter in marriage, the groom's family offers gifts to the family of the bride intended for the young couple as a hedge against any future inclination toward divorce on the part of the husband. The newlyweds often live in an apartment adjacent to the bride's family home, and the wedding festivities begin when the families dedicate the new residence the night before the marriage itself. In the morning the couple offer food to gathered monks, and in return a monk purifies the house with sprinkled water. An ablution ceremony for the couple occurs that afternoon, with the guests passing the seated newlyweds and pouring some water over them from a ceremonial conch shell. After serving tea, the couple receive gifts from their well-wishers. A lengthy dinner celebration is prelude to a ceremony in which an older married couple make the new marriage bed. Guests impart their blessings and all depart.

Because Buddhists generally regard marriage as a nonreligious ritual, the involvement of monks is fairly minimal even in a predominantly Buddhist country like Thailand and only in the preparatory stages of the rite. No official representative of Buddhism presides over or witnesses the contract at the core of the wedding ceremony; that is the function of all the invited guests. In countries like China and Japan, where Buddhism exists alongside strong indigenous traditions such as Daoism and Shinto, weddings are frequently within the purview of the indigenous tradition. An interesting feature of Buddhist practice evidenced in the early sources is that one or both of the partners might choose to enter the monastic sangha after marriage. A wife needed her husband's permission to do so, but some women became nuns when their husbands decided to become monks or at the death of a husband. Early tradition appears to have discouraged remarriage.

As for divorce, practice among Buddhists today varies, and just as marriage between Buddhists is generally a civil matter, so is divorce. However, early tradition specified several limits. Adultery or other forms of infidelity was sufficient cause for either partner to divorce the other. Beyond that the wife had no right to initiate divorce, but the husband could divorce his wife on the grounds of infertility or incompatibility. This marks an advance for women over prevailing Hindu custom, which allowed a husband to divorce a wife merely because of disobedience, unproductive labor, or chronic illness or because she bore him only daughters.

88. What do the classic Buddhist sources say about "family values"?

A text of the Pali Canon tells a marvelous tale about how the Buddha encountered a youth named Singala who made a practice of paying homage to the six directions (the four cardinal points plus up and down). Now, the Teacher said, understand the real meaning of the six directions; and he proceeded to associate each with a specific set of relationships. The correspondences reveal a lot about early Buddhist social and family values. To the east are one's parents, whose task is to guide their children, encourage them in constructive occupations, educate and see that they are well married, and leave them an inheritance. Children must revere their parents, with special morning, noon, and evening gestures; care for them as they grow old; uphold family honor; keep their wealth intact; and bury them according to sacred tradition. In the west one finds the spousal bond. Children also look to the south where the Buddha places teachers, working assiduously and respectfully in return for competent instruction and the teacher's help in seeking employment.

Toward the west, husband and wife must have the highest respect for each other, safeguarding their mutual fidelity and fulfilling a range of obligations. Let the husband love and honor his wife unstintingly, see to her comfort and security, and offer her what luxuries he can afford. For her part the wife takes care of the home, entertains visitors of all kinds, loves her spouse faithfully, and exercises stewardship over their resources. Husbands are told to have a "mother-mind" or "daughter-mind" or "sister-mind" toward women other than their wives, depending on their age, as a safeguard to chastity. To the north the Buddha located relatives, along with friends and neighbors, a kind of extended family. Charity and hospitality are the key virtues in this instance, along with civility, mutual support, avoidance of conflict, assistance in difficulty, and constancy.

The father of a family may in addition have dealings with employees to whom he owes reasonable tasks and fair wages and medical coverage, along with rewards for special competence, even though employees are at the nadir. Finally, at the apex, all members of the family relate to the monastic members of the sangha generously and respectfully, in return for the monk or nun's sharing knowledge and moral leadership. As for individual roles within the family, tradition has a good deal to say about those of mother and daughter. The place of mothers in Buddhist society has been somewhat ambiguous. On the one hand, motherhood confers authority; on the other, motherhood carries a certain stigma associated with sexual activity, from which only the mothers of Buddhas and bodhisattvas are free. Mothers are described as like bodhisattvas in the way they feel compassion for their children, but only the ideal mother, Maya, experienced anything like the sublime freedom of a bodhisattva. In the traditional teaching, daughters must follow the example of their mothers in curbing their carnal weakness.

89.   Birth seems to be a major element in the Buddhist notion of suffering. Is birth a cause for blaming women? Is there rejoicing in a Buddhist family when a child is born?

There is a profound paradox here. On the one hand, birth, the phenomenon of sentient beings begetting offspring out of desire of various kinds, is one of the 12 links in the chain of conditioned origination. A person who dies unliberated from desire is frankly condemned to coming around again. Strictly speaking, one cannot achieve liberation without breaking the endless cycle, and that suggests that birth is anything but a blessing. In some places, such as Japan, Buddhism has come to be associated far more with death and funerals than with birth. Japanese couples take their newborn children to a Shinto shrine for a blessing, a ritual that is in effect missing from the Buddhist liturgical repertoire.

On the other hand, Buddhist families everywhere celebrate the arrival of new life in their midst with great rejoicing. Even if parents-to-be are devout practitioners of the faith, they are not likely to castigate themselves as religiously lax because they are expecting a child. Nor will they likely be ready to simply throw up their hands with a gesture of hopelessness, and say, "That's life. Whadya gonna do?" Devout Buddhists who reflect seriously on the human condition can find much in their tradition that blends compassion with hard-headed realism. In the end, one has to deal with what one is given, and Buddhism offers a way to see it through in hope.

NINE:

BUDDHISM HERE AND NOW

90. Has the fast pace of modernity taken its toll on Buddhism as it has on other ancient faith traditions?

Effects of secularism, commodity-mongering, profit motive, and the headlong lunge for scientific certitude have indeed taken their toll on Buddhism. But the tradition has become part of so many and such diverse cultures that it is very difficult to characterize the situation in a thumbnail sketch. Perhaps a glimpse at the place of Buddhism in Japanese society will offer at least some idea. There is a saying in Japan that has made it into English as "Shinto marries, Buddhism buries." The common reference to "funeral Buddhism" (*shoshiki bukkyo*) is hardly a ringing endorsement for the tradition's vitality in Japanese life. Young parents with their newborns and business partners who are just beginning a new venture go to Shinto shrines for a blessing, and celebrations of initiations of every sort, including that of the New Year, are associated with Shinto. At the other end of life, most funerals are Buddhist, and nearly every Buddhist temple has a small cemetery on the adjoining property.

But the story of Japanese Buddhism is not altogether lugubrious. Buddhism in all its variety remains an important element in the lives of millions of Japanese. Many Japanese continue to engage in religious practices associated with both Shinto and Buddhism for different reasons and on different occasions. Even in Tokyo and other large cities, many Buddhist temples still attract throngs of worshipers seeking to be healed and strengthened spiritually. At places like Tokyo's Asakusa Kannon temple, people cleanse themselves symbolically by waving puffs of incense from an enormous cauldron toward them and then rubbing their faces with its vapors, among other popular devotional practices. Significant numbers of devotees still gather in large temples to chant and individuals still seek solitude and meditative discipline in hundreds of monastery temples.

Buddhism's situation varies enormously from country to country. In the People's Republic of China, the Maoist era inflicted massive damage on Buddhism at every level. The newest generation of Chinese know

145

little or nothing of Buddhism or of religion in general; surviving monasteries and temples struggle to hang on or function as museumlike show pieces. On the island of Taiwan, Buddhism has fared somewhat better, but many temples there are syncretistic, blending elements of Buddhism and popular Daoism with miscellaneous folk traditions. Buddha and the various bodhisattvas, especially Kwan Yin, find themselves surrounded by effigies of ancestor deities and gods of wealth and literature. Buddhism has become too integral to the cultures of Asia to disappear entirely, and some scholars see signs of change injecting new vitality into Buddhist communities both in Asia and elsewhere.

91. Is there any sort of global Buddhist organization that claims to speak for all Buddhists?

The World Fellowship of Buddhists originated in Sri Lanka (Ceylon) in 1950 as a result of a congress attended by representatives of virtually every Buddhist lineage. Its stated goals are to encourage practice of Buddha's teachings and correct ritual observance, to promote world Buddhist unity, to carry out a global teaching ministry, to sponsor various humanitarian undertakings, and to work toward universal peace and harmony. Representatives from various geographical regions make up a general council, which in turn appoints a board of trustees to administer its holdings. In addition the fellowship has an executive council made up of an elected president, 12 vice-presidents, and chairpersons of various standing committees (finance, publicity and education, dharma propagation, youth, and humanitarian services), along with an honorary general secretary and an honorary treasurer. Answering to the general council, the executive council delegates operational responsibilities to one or more of its members who reside in the nation that is currently hosting the fellowship's headquarters. The organization has held international meetings every two or three years since its inception to discuss issues of universal interest and in the hope of fostering worldwide cooperation among Buddhism's many organizations and sects. The fellowship claims no definitive teaching authority but actively seeks reconciliation among the various interest groups when disagreements arise. Its secretariat is currently located in Bangkok, Thailand.

92. Who is the Dalai Lama, and why does he seem to be so important for many Buddhists? Is he something like a Buddhist pope?

Tenzin Gyatso (1935–), referred to as *his holiness,* is the fourteenth Dalai Lama ("ocean [of knowledge] religious teacher") in the Gelug-pa, or Yellow Hat, Tibetan Buddhist lineage. His tradition holds that the Buddha-nature is reincarnated endlessly in certain chosen individuals whose coming is foretold and who manifest certain signs on their bodies soon after birth. The thirteenth Dalai Lama died in 1933, and for the next several years, leaders of the Gelug-pa order searched for candidates who passed various tests stipulated by the tradition. Of three possible infants, one emerged as a clear choice and in 1940 was brought to Lhasa's seventeenth-century Potala Palace in Tibet to begin his regime. The five-year-old boy underwent lengthy training in meditative disciplines, elaborate chanting and ritual practice, and philosophy under the order's special tutors. When the Chinese invaded Tibet in 1950, the young lama reached his religious majority prematurely as a result of the crisis. Conditions in Tibet deteriorated under increasing Chinese repression, so the Dalai Lama fled to India in 1959 and has lived there ever since.

A widely held view claims the Dalai Lama as the official political leader and spokesperson of Tibet's Buddhists, including even many not associated with his lineage. Another prominent figure called the Panchen Lama has been Tibet's spiritual leader. Though he holds no special standing for other Buddhist denominations, millions of people of many faiths admire and perhaps even revere Tenzin Gyatso as a genuinely wise and holy man who embodies the best of Buddhist values. The Dalai Lama won the Nobel Prize for Peace in 1989 and has written a number of books now translated into various languages.

93. How is Buddhism becoming "inculturated" in the United States?

Honolulu has been a sort of gateway city for Buddhism's entry to the United States, and the Soto Mission on Nuuanu Street offers an excellent example of several important aspects of Buddhist inculturation in an American context. The mission temple, built in 1952, is an attractive building. Clearly not a church, its central spirelike tower is very Indian in style, recalling the tall structure that marks the place of Buddha's Enlightenment at Bodhgaya, not far from Banaras. Walk inside and look toward the altar, and you might think you are in Japan, but the benches look suspiciously like church pews, right down to the hymnal racks. Flip through a hymnal and you know you're in the U.S.A. Set to a tune familiar to many Christians are the words, "Buddha loves me, this I know, 'cause the Sutra tells me so."

Missionaries of the Soto Zen lineage first established a branch in Hawaii in 1913. They have since opted for an approach to inculturation that integrates architectural reminiscences of Buddhism's Indian origins and Soto Zen's Japanese roots with American Christian elements of community and (Sunday) ritual, even including the office of bishop in their authority structure. In a similar vein, missionaries of Japan's True Pure Land lineage (Jodoshinshu) have organized their efforts under the name of the Buddhist Churches of America, referring to their worship leaders as ministers.

Not all forms of Buddhism have attempted to inculturate themselves to this extent. Many lineages, such as those of Tibetan Vajrayana, for example, retain more of the ritual "feel" of their pre-American forms. About a half-million Buddhists now live in the U.S.A. That total includes an increasing number of indigenous converts to the tradition, especially into the Zen and Vajrayana (Tibetan) lineages. Immigrants by and large make up the memberships of various other Chinese and Japanese Mahayana lineages, especially Pure Land and True Pure Land groups, and of Theravada temples serving southeast Asians largely by national origin.

94. Can a non-Buddhist attend a Buddhist service? What sort of etiquette should one observe when visiting a Buddhist temple?

Many, perhaps even most, Buddhist temples welcome non-Buddhists. Larger, more well-established temples often post announcements in local newspapers as to their schedule of services. It is appropriate to call ahead to ask whether visitors are welcome at a given religious observance. Visitors are free to participate in communal rituals as they wish. Major ritual activities include offering incense, chanting texts from the Sutras or singing hymns, and quiet meditation. Guests who choose not to participate should observe in silence from the back or side of the temple. Rituals in most well-established temples are led by a priest or monk, but a lay member of the community can also lead in the absence of an official minister.

In addition to their regular weekly or even daily prayer and meditation rituals, temples also accommodate a variety of other special rituals to which guests might be invited. These include ceremonies marking the initiation of new members of the Buddhist community, weddings (typically in the form of a Protestant Christian ceremony), wakes and funerals. Other celebrations of regular festivities in the Buddhist liturgical calendar include the Buddha's birthday on April 8; the remembrance of Buddha's enlightenment on December 8; and observance of Buddha's entry into final nirvana on February 15. Some temple services include a passing of the plate for offerings, but more often visitors will find an offering box near the entrance of the temple where they can make a small donation as they wish.

95. Have there been significant reform movements in modern times? Does the cult known as Aum Shinrikyo have any connection with Buddhism?

A number of modern organizations have Buddhist roots, especially in postwar Japan. Many Japanese, disillusioned with the ineffectiveness of mainline Buddhist lineages and temples, welcomed the new movements. Among the most important are those associated with Nichiren, especially Soka Gakkai, an organization that has sought to renew the thirteenth-century Nichiren Shoshu ("Nichiren True Teaching"). Soka Gakkai ("Society for the Creation of Values") began in 1937 as a lay movement to spread the teaching of Nichiren, emphasizing the preeminence of practical results over doctrinal content. After World War II, Soka Gakkai remobilized and launched a campaign of energetic proselytizing called "break and subdue" (*shakubuku*). Conversions to the sect increased dramatically. The central ritual is twice daily chanting of the phrase "*nam myoho renge kyo*" ("Homage to the Lotus of the Good Law Sutra") along with other texts from that scripture. The purpose of the chanting is to internalize and embody the fullness of the Lotus Sutra, thereby transforming the self and eventually all of society through its salvific teachings.

Soka Gakkai and several other twentieth-century movements related to the Nichiren lineage, such as Reiyukai and Rissho Koseikai (further discussed in Question 96), have sought to reorient Buddhist teaching away from what they consider ineffectual doctrine by focusing on major social and economic issues. They have appealed to working-class people and in recent years worked to secure their goals by engaging in the political process directly. Reiyukai ("Spiritual Friends Association"), added a distinctive view that rites of ancestor veneration were the duty not of the clergy but of the laity. One of Reiyukai's most prominent leaders was a woman named Kotani Kimi who has even been hailed as Miroku, the Japanese Maitreya or Buddha of the Future (see Question 101). Common characteristics of all these groups, in addition to their roots in the Nichiren tradition, are social activism and establishment of a Buddhist lay authority structure independent of the monastic institution.

Aum Shinrikyo, much in the news during the late 1990s in connection with alleged attempts to introduce poison gas into the Tokyo subway system, is not an offshoot of Buddhism but of Shinto, Japan's most important indigenous religious tradition. Like a number of other Shinto-derived sects (such as Tenrikyo and Kurozumikyo), it centers on a charismatic leader either identified as divine or believed to be possessed by a deity.

96. Has Buddhism been especially important in modern peace movements?

Buddhists the world over have espoused the cause of global peace, and some have committed themselves to it as a personal vocation. The Dalai Lama is perhaps the single best-known Buddhist peace activist, but there are a number of organizations dedicated to peace as well. Several years ago, a group of Japanese Buddhists, along with several U.S. companions, came through St. Louis on their way from California to New York in a walk for world peace. They contacted me and asked if they could come and speak to my class on Religious Traditions of Asia. They began with several minutes of chanting, repeating the phrase "*nam myoho renge kyo*," ("Homage to the Lotus of the Good Law Sutra). Then they explained their connection with Nichiren Shoshu and initiated a very animated discussion about the need for world peace based on the teachings of the Buddha and of their founding figure, Nichiren, and his disciple Nikko. Their goal, they explained, was to bring about a total transformation of human society in order to lay the groundwork for global peace.

Another Japanese organization much involved in peace activism is called Rissho Koseikai ("Society Establishing Righteousness and Harmony"), and it too is connected with Nichiren Shoshu. Dissatisfied with traditional Buddhism's concern with values that they deemed too detached from immediate experience, Rissho Koseikai's postwar leadership shifted its focus to the quest for world peace through understanding among religious traditions. In this respect this movement is very different from the highly nationalistic Reiyukai, which has called for recision of the clause in the Japanese constitution that enshrines an official anti-war policy. Reiyukai has even called for government sponsorship of Yasukuni Jinja, an important Shinto shrine in Tokyo that honors those who died in World War II.

97. There has been increasing interest lately, among Christians at least, in the connections between spirituality and health. Does Buddhism have anything to say about that?

Buddhist teaching addresses itself first and foremost to what ails humankind and all sentient beings—suffering in all its forms. Enlightenment is virtually synonymous with healing; in that sense, Buddhism is all about spirituality as a source of healing. Various subsects have developed around the idea of healing at different times and places in the history of Buddhism. Japanese tradition, for example, acknowledges one aspect of the Buddha and two bodhisattvas whose sole work is healing. The Buddha called Yakushi-Nyorai descended, mythically speaking, from the Tibetan Bhaishajyaguru ("Master of Healing" in Sanskrit) who taught the sages the arts of medicine. Still a popular object of veneration in Japan, this luminous "great king of physicians" is completely dedicated to attending the sick. The bodhisattvas Yaku-o and Yakujo represent ancient personifications of the imminent and accessible power of healing.

Buddhists can choose from a wide variety of specific methods of spiritual healing. Silent meditation is at once the most basic and the most advanced healing technique, aimed at ultimately freeing the individual practitioner from the bonds of craving and the pain of life's muddle and confusion. Various forms of scriptural chanting and the use of mantras add an oral-aural dimension. Vocal prayer can include direct supplication of the healing Buddha and bodhisattvas as well. There is also a rich visual dimension to Buddhism's healing resources. Much of Buddhist art is meant to assist the meditator in visualizing the healing powers and the path that leads to the alleviation of suffering.

Buddhist sources from ancient times have always dealt with diverse physical means of healing, such as herbal remedies, diet, surgery, and a wide range of bodily therapies. But what is most important to note about Buddhism's various approaches to spiritual healing is the underlying conviction that attitude and belief have a great deal to do with every kind of illness. Ignorance and negative thinking are primary causes of malaise at every level of existence. The more an appreciation of the power of the mind–body connection informs contemporary medical practice in nontraditional societies such as those of the United States and Europe, the more we who live in those societies may come to appreciate the wisdom of the Buddhist tradition in this respect.

98. Are there any distinctively Buddhist views on environmental issues?

Many contemporary Buddhists regard their founder's teachings as pioneering insights into the essential relationships between human beings and the rest of the material world. Three aspects of those teachings are especially relevant here. First, the Buddha's largely psychological approach, in which the knowing subject and the known object are intimately connected, underscores both the spiritual implications of environmental problems and the environmental impact of spiritual malaise. For example, hopelessness arises out of the exploitation of natural resources by the wealthy, while uncontrolled grasping after wealth and power give rise to the abuse of nature, and so on in a vicious cycle. Only a proper perspective on the nature of the human situation can lead to sane policies on environmental questions.

Second, Buddhist compassion is the basis, not only for an attitude of global toleration of religious and cultural diversity, but for a sense of unity with all living things. Seeing to it that every creature has its basic rights upheld is in the long-term interests of all, for all things are inextricably joined in a universal web of life. Hence environmental issues are inseparably linked with social issues so that violence against nature is violence against persons, and vice versa. As in all its teachings, here too Buddhism emphasizes the ultimate goal of liberation from suffering at every level of existence. Humanity's hope is an increasing awareness that one can be reasonably content with a great deal less than the strident voices of our materialistic cultures would have us think.

Finally, Buddhism's concept of skill in means seeks to ensure that we enact our compassion wisely. This means first of all seeking "right livelihood" as a way of earning one's wealth and accepting full responsibility for the consequences of one's choices. Earth's environment suffers more daily as a result of unregulated exploitation on a large scale and the refusal to accept the reality that all of our individual choices matter on the smaller scale. Any means of livelihood that gains wealth for the few at the expense of the many is clearly unacceptable. Skill in means looks not only to the immediate requirements of a particular task, but to the long range effects as well. Because all problems begin with individual attitudes, Buddhist teaching counsels that each person take account of his or her inner dispositions through meditation. Only individual awareness of the issues by growing numbers of persons holds any serious hope of change.

99. What languages do specialists in Buddhist studies need to learn?

Choice of a primary language for the study of Buddhism is not quite so obvious as for concentrations in Islam, Judaism, Confucianism, Shinto, or Hinduism. Arabic, Hebrew, Chinese, Japanese, and Sanskrit are the chief first languages of specialists in those traditions because they remain their respective scriptural and liturgical tongues. Buddhism began as a tradition in which use of vernacular languages even for more or less official religious purposes, such as recitation of scripture, was not only acceptable but assumed. Strictly speaking, therefore, Buddhism has no canonical language. One might presume that because Buddhism and Hinduism originated in India, one would need more or less the same languages for both. But at least two interesting circumstances have resulted in the divergence of linguistic histories and, thus, of modern scholarly pathways through the Buddhist and Hindu traditions.

Though both traditions witnessed the development of successive "layers" of scriptural texts, the Hindu scriptures were almost exclusively in Sanskrit. Earliest Buddhist canonical scriptures were first written down in one of the "Prakrits," a Sanskrit-related vernacular called Pali, and was also written in the Devanagari script. Later canons of Buddhist scripture were however composed in Sanskrit or Buddhist Hybrid Sanskrit. Second, though a number of other languages have gradually assumed importance for scholars of Hinduism, they are virtually all Indic. Buddhist tradition, on the other hand, now virtually vanished from the land of its origin, was translated into nearly a dozen other east and southeast Asian languages as it followed its missionary path over the Himalayas.

One result of Buddhism's becoming so thoroughly inculturated into Tibet, Korea, China, Japan, and the nations formerly called Indo-China, for example, is that scholars virtually have to specialize in one type of Buddhism as manifested in a single region with its chief language, with perhaps a subspecialization in a second canonical tongue. For example, a scholar of Theravada Buddhism might work with Pali in addition to one or more regional southeast Asian languages such as Thai, Vietnamese, Laotian, or Khmer; a specialist in Korean or Japanese Buddhism might choose to learn some Chinese because so many Korean and Japanese texts were translated from Chinese versions; or a scholar of Vajrayana or Chinese Pure Land might study Sanskrit to supplement a principal focus on Tibetan or Chinese, because many Chinese and Tibetan texts were translated directly from Sanskrit canonical texts. In addition, a specialist's option for a particular historical period will make nearly as much difference as will the choice of geographical region.

100. What do you personally—I mean beyond your being a professional student of religion—think of Buddhism? Perhaps I'm really asking how you "feel" about it.

Of the various religious traditions I have had the luxury of studying, none seems to be so often accepted as unthreatening by members of other traditions as Buddhism. While traveling in Korea in 1983, I had several experiences that impressed on me Buddhism's uncanny ability to play the part of a revered presence in society even for members of another faith community. After attending the priestly ordination of a Korean Jesuit friend, the new priest invited me to join his family for a day of sightseeing around Seoul. They did not get to the capital often

and wanted to make the rounds of some of Korea's major cultural treasures. As we entered the National Palace Museum, we made our way to
the Buddhist art galleries. At one end of the large Buddha room was a
seated image of the Enlightened One that had been at least informally
designated as the museum's "shrine" image. On his lap, many passing
museum patrons had left offerings of currency. Our group moved to
view the many works of religious sculpture, but the young priest's
Catholic mother and aunt had a ritual stop to make. Standing before the
designated Buddha, both bowed reverently, prayed briefly, and left a
small offering. When I asked the Korean Jesuit about it, he simply
smiled and said, "Everybody here loves the Buddha."

Several days later, an elderly Korean Jesuit kindly offered to go
with me to a famous Son (Korean for Zen) temple called Toson-sa,
perched on a hill overlooking Seoul. In the taxi on the way, my guide
talked at length, animatedly, and with obvious depth of feeling about
Buddhism. What a wonderful contribution to humanity Buddhism continued to make, he observed from several angles, unlike traditional
Korean shamanism which he roundly dismissed as so much charlatanry.
After we arrived at Toson-sa, we were walking by the small building
housing the cells of the resident monks when a monk emerged. The
Jesuit and the monk exchanged greetings, and the Jesuit asked me if I
would like to speak with the monk while he translated for us. Absolutely,
I answered, and popped my first question. Back and forth went our
translated exchanges for 10 minutes or so, but gradually, as if completely enchanted by what the monk had to say, the Jesuit forgot to translate. The Catholic and the Buddhist, total strangers prior to that day,
were engaging each other with great amusement and, I found out later,
exchanging views about the glories and frailties of human nature.

Perhaps these instances of such an amicable Catholic response to
Buddhism were more a function of the warmth and expressive nature of
these particular Koreans than any particular quality of Buddhism. Perhaps not, for I observed similar reactions from Catholic acquaintances in
Japan and Taiwan as well. I have found myself very much attracted to
various aspects of East Asian Buddhism in a similar way over the years.
What I have noticed most about Buddhism is that there is a welcoming
gentleness about its public presence. One could no doubt multiply
instances in which Buddhists have made public nuisances of themselves

or advanced causes obnoxious to their neighbors, but my own experience has been of another order altogether.

101.   Have you ever felt anything like a personal spiritual connection with Buddhism?

For many years my favorite work of religious sculpture was Michelangelo's most famous *Pieta*. When I first visited Japan, in June 1983, the Florentine's masterpiece met its match. Ever since I first began to study Buddhism, I had been thoroughly enamored of its art, and a top priority was to make a visit to Koryuji, one of Kyoto's oldest temples. Legend, if not hard fact, associated the temple with emperor Shotoku Taishi, who had been instrumental in welcoming Buddhism to Japan. More importantly, Koryuji's most treasured object was a modest wooden statue, perhaps 4 feet tall, of the bodhisattva Miroku (a Korean-Japanese version of Maitreya, a name that means "Loving One").

Miroku no longer occupied a place on a temple altar where devotees might pray for guidance. Now the statue was on display at the center of the temple's modern "treasure house," a small museum. As the pneumatic door slid open, I entered to find all the temple's most prized religious sculptures arrayed on a raised platform that stretched along the side and rear walls. Centered along the back wall was the Miroku. The few other visitors ambled quietly, reverently, appreciating the serene images of Buddha, the benevolent bodhisattvas, and the fearsome guardian figures that once glowered menacingly down on the temple's entry portals. I wanted to go straight to the Miroku but decided to save the best for last.

As I walked toward the platform along the right wall, I heard the sound of buses arriving, and the crescendo chirping of a hundred small field-tripping children approaching the automatic doors. Teachers struggled for the attention of their charges now lost in the magical squeak of sneakers on polished cypress. To my great relief, the instructor finished his presentation, and the sound of the diesel-borne throng receded. The perfect moment arrived as I found myself alone in the splendid space. I sat against a pillar and looked up and slightly to the right at the face of Miroku, inclining gracefully toward me. Most of the original pigments were now worn away, revealing a mellow grain in the red Korean pine. I

moved to another pillar and sat looking up at Miroku's left side, relishing the silent averted glance, the ageless beauty.

From off in the distance the sound of buses intruded again. Scores of squeaking sneakers surrounded me in minutes and I resented the children for shattering my silence. I would surrender my pillar to the crowd and return to it when they left. As my fit of selfishness melted away with the sound of the departing children, I realized that this ancient presence was there not for me alone, but to gaze with eternal compassion on the ceaseless ebb and flow of a humanity so needy for all its wealth.

June 18, 1988. I walked into the front hall of a Jesuit house to begin a retreat. There on the wall hung a beautiful framed image of the Koryuji Miroku that the director of the house had brought from Kyoto a few years earlier. That evening I pulled out a copy of Rosemary Haughton's *The Passionate God*. I had read it some years earlier and wanted to read it again, not recalling that it had been my companion in Japan in 1983. As I opened the volume, the bookmark slipped into my hand, a picture of Miroku emerging from five years of dark confinement. Now two images of the bodhisattva, viewed as though from the vantage point of my two pillars, look down from above my desk. Thoughts of Miroku's carefree children move me still, reminders of the boundless compassion at the heart of a world-treasure called Buddhism.

CHART OF MAJOR BUDDHIST LINEAGES

Early Indian Schools

The Sthaviravadins: Although not formal lineages, these early followers of the Buddha should be classified as Theravadins. They find their philosophical point of departure in the teaching that the self or ego is merely a loose grouping of impermanent and ever-changing aggregates. The end of such teaching was to assert that everything is transient and that one should not become attached to selves or other objects.

The Sarvastivadins: This group contended that "everything exists," including all past, present, and future happenings, in spite of there being no existent self or ego. The combination of all things according to one's *karma* brings about one's state of consciousness. The group was declared heretical by most other Buddhist lineages.

China

Mahayana Schools Imported from India

San Lun or Madhyamika: Based on the Chinese translation of Nagarjuna's (second century) *Madhyamika Karika* and two other works of uncertain authorship, this lineage emphasized the notions of *shunyata* (emptiness) and *wu* (nonbeing). So rigorous was the teaching of this lineage that it declared that the elements constituting perceived objects, when examined, are really no more than mental phenomena and have no true existence.

159

Yogacara: Founded in the third century by Maitreyanatha and made famous by Asanga and Vasubandhu in the fourth or fifth century, this school held that the source of all ideas is *vijñana* ("consciousness"), which is seen as the fundamental basis of experience. Ultimate reality is therefore only perceived but has no real existence.

Indigenous Mahayana Lineages

T'ien T'ai: Named after the mountain on which its founder Zhi Yi (d. 597) resided, this lineage is based on a scheme of classification intended to integrate and harmonize the vast array of Buddhist scriptures and doctrines. This scheme of classification is based on the Buddhist doctrine of *upaya* ("skill in means"). The most important form of Buddhism for this lineage is the Mahayana devotionalism found in the *Lotus Sutra.*

Hua Yen or Avatamsaka: This lineage takes its name from the *Avatamsaka Sutra,* its central sacred text, and like the T'ien T'ai school is oriented toward a classification of sutras. Basic to this lineage is the assertion that all particulars are merely manifestations of the absolute mind and are therefore fundamentally the same.

Ching T'u or Pure Land: Based on the *Sukhavati Vyuha* ("Pure Land Sutra"), this lineage was founded in 402 by Hui Yuan. The Pure Land lineage held that the spiritual quality of the world had been in decline since its height during the lifetime of the Buddha and taught followers to cultivate through prayer and devotion a sincere intent to be reborn in the heavenly paradise of the Buddha Amitabha.

Ch'an: Its name derived from the Sanskrit term *dhyana* ("meditation"), this lineage emphasized meditation as the only means to a spiritual awakening beyond words or thought, dispensing almost entirely with the teachings and practices of traditional Buddhism. Ch'an Buddhism is thought to have been brought to China by the enigmatic Indian monk Bodhidharma in about the year 500. Salvation is primarily a personal experience, although emphasis is also laid on the master-disciple relationship in attaining an insight into one's own true nature and thus attaining Buddhahood. Two of the most important Ch'an schools are the Ts'ao-tung ("Five

Ranks"), founded by I-hsuan (d. 867), which emphasized the attainment of enlightenment through a program of meditation that can last many years; and the Lin-chi ("Shouting and Striking") school founded by Liang-chieh (d. 869), which held that one could attain more immediate results through the use of arresting methods designed to shock the aspirant out of dependence on linear thinking.

Japan

Tendai: (Chinese T'ien T'ai) Founded in Japan by Saicho (d. 822), this lineage quickly rose to prominence as the most important lineage of Japanese Buddhism. The basic doctrines of this lineage and the Chinese T'ien T'ai are the same, as is their reverence for the *Lotus Sutra*, but Tendai differs in its emphasis on the mystical and esoteric aspects of Buddhism. The four primary categories of this lineage are (1) morality, (2) monastic discipline, (3) esoteric practices, and (4) meditation.

Shingon: Founded by Kukai (d. 835), this lineage grew to rival the Tendai lineage as early as the late ninth century. The Shingon belief system was tantric and taught that through mantras (short, repetitive incantations or prayers), meditation, and the performance of hand gestures one can gain access to the power of the Buddhas and bodhisattvas.

Jodo or Pure Land: Begun at the time of publication of the treatise by Honen (d. 1212) entitled *Senchaku-shu,* this lineage traces its scriptural heritage to the *Pure Land Sutra (Sukhavati Vyuha),* which prescribes loving devotion to the Buddha Amida as a means to be reborn in the Pure Land, or the paradise over which he presides. Pure Land prayer centers on the repetition of the phrase *namu amida butsu* ("Homage to Amida Buddha") and became one of the most popular forms of Buddhism in Japan.

Joho Shinshu or True Pure Land: Founded by Shinran (d. 1262), this lineage takes Pure Land teaching one step further, claiming that humility and faith in Amida's love are in themselves true signs that the redeeming grace of the Buddha has already been bestowed. Amida Buddha seeks and saves without first requiring faith and good works. These spring up spontaneously from Amida's spiritual presence in the heart.

Nichiren: Named after its founder Nichiren (d. 1282), this lineage was founded on the *Lotus Sutra* and taught that mere repetition of the title of that sutra *Nam-myoho-renge-kyo* ("Homage to the Lotus Sutra") was sufficient to gain one access to paradise.

Zen: The monk Eisai (d. 1215) is usually considered the first proponent of Zen in Japan, although Ch'an had existed since the early sixth century and probably existed also in Japan before Eisai's time. The earliest forms of Zen generally avoided intellectualism and deemphasized scriptures, doctrine, and ceremonial. Eisai, whose form of Zen took on the name Rinzai (Lin-chi, Ch.) affirmed the authority of the traditional Buddhist scriptures and used the koan or meditational riddle as a means of transcending linear thinking. Soto Zen (Ts'ao-tung, Ch.), tracing its roots back to Dogen (d. 1253), also affirmed the validity of the Buddhist scriptures but de-emphasized the use of koans and focused solely on extended, silent meditation.

Tibet

Nyingma-pa: Tracing its origins to the legendary Padma-sambhava, an eighth-century Tantric magician, this lineage of Buddhism is uniquely Tibetan in that many aspects of traditional Bon religion are mixed together with more properly Buddhist beliefs and practices to form a unique expression of Buddhist piety. This lineage emphasizes the move toward more advanced stages of enlightenment through "preliminary practices" that comprise the beliefs and practices of Buddhism before the advent of Tantra, and through "higher practices," which involve the attainment of enlightenment through the chanting of magical spells, special hand gestures, mystical diagrams, and ritualized sexual intercourse.

Gelug-pa: Founded by Tsong-kha-pa (d. 1419) as a reform movement within Tibetan Buddhism, followers acclaimed the lineage's third teacher as an incarnation of the bodhisattva Avalokiteshvara, thus inaugurating the line of Dalai Lamas, the fourteenth and most recent of whom was born in 1935. Emphasis in this lineage is on a strict monastic discipline and on the conviction that the bodhisattva, a Buddha who has foregone final nirvana out of compassion for all sentient beings, is continually present.

SELECT GLOSSARY OF BUDDHIST SANSKRIT/PALI TECHNICAL TERMS

Arhat/arahat: perfected spiritual seeker, typically a member of the monastic *sangha* who has achieved freedom from the cycles of rebirth; the Theravada ideal.

Anatman/anatta: "nonself, no-soul," the Buddhist negation of the Hindu understanding of *atman* as indestructible core of personal individuality.

Anittya/anicca: "impermanence," one of the three essential characteristics of existence, along with *anatman* and *duhkha.*

Bhikshu(ni)/bhikku(ni): male (female) mendicant, "beggar," referring to monks and nuns.

Bodhisattva: "enlightenment-being," the ideal of spiritual attainment especially in Mahayana traditions; one who forgoes final entry into nirvana out of compassion for all sentient beings.

Buddha: fully "enlightened one," a historical person in the Theravada view; one of innumerable beings in Mahayana views because each person is a potential buddha.

Buddhi: intuitive awareness, true intelligence, that mental faculty capable of profoundest insight.

Dharma/dhamma: core teachings of the Buddha, the sum of qualities of mundane existence.

165

Duhkha/dukkha: sorrow, sadness, dissatisfaction with the way things are, a central factor in the human condition, one of the "three marks" of existence.

Dhyana/jhana: meditation, concentration.

Karma/kamma: "action," the cosmic law of cause and effect: every physical or spiritual deed has its long-range consequences as determined by the agent's intention.

Karuna: compassion for all sentient beings, what motivates a *bodhisattva.*

Mandala: "circle," a key design element in Buddhist art, symbol of inward spiritual realities.

Mantra: a spiritually potent formula, often of only one or two syllables, used in certain Buddhist rituals.

Mudra: hand gesture, essential element in Buddhist iconography.

Nirvana/nibbana: "no-wind/breath," final goal for Buddhists representing definitive liberation from the cycle of rebirth.

Pagoda: typically an east-Asian multistoried memorial structure, ultimately derived from an elaboration of the upper portions of a *stupa.*

Prajña/pañña: pure and intuitive "wisdom," one of the aspects under which the goal of Buddhism is known, often personified as feminine.

Roshi: Japanese term for a Zen master, sometimes functioning as abbot of a monastery.

Samadhi: absorption yielding final liberation, the ultimate goal of Buddhist spiritual practice.

Samsara: the world of appearances and endless flux, including all aspects of becoming and death; cycles of birth and rebirth.

Sangha: "assembly, community," usually referring to the Buddhist order of monks and nuns.

Satori: Japanese term for full enlightenment.

Skandha: "aggregate," one of the five constituents of the construct called "personality."

Shunyata/sunnata: "emptiness, void," the ultimate meaning of all things as a result of the three "features of existence," suffering, impermanence, and no-soul.

Stupa: a earthen mound surmounted by a solid square topped by conical spire (hence associated with original meaning of "hairknot"), originally used to enshrine relics of the Buddha.

Sutra/sutta: "thread," major category of Buddhist scripture.

Vipashyana/vipassana: "penetrating insight" into the three marks of existence; a term often applied to the practice of meditation in some Mahayana traditions.

Zazen: Japanese term for "sitting-absorption," meditative Zen practice.

SUGGESTIONS FOR FURTHER READING

Aitken, Molly Emma, ed. *Meeting the Buddha: On Pilgrimage in Buddhist India*. New York: Riverhead Books, 1995.

Birnbaum, Raoul. *The Healing Buddha*. Boulder, Colo.: Shambhala, 1979.

Boucher, Sandy. *Turning the Wheel: American Women Creating the New Buddhism*. Boston: Beacon Press, 1993.

_____. *Opening the Lotus: A Woman's Guide to Buddhism*. Boston: Beacon Press, 1997.

Ch'en, Kenneth. *The Chinese Transformation of Buddhism*. Princeton, N.J.: Princeton University Press, 1973.

Corless, Roger. *The Vision of Buddhism*. New York: Paragon House, 1989.

Dumoulin, Heinrich, S.J. *Zen Buddhism: a History*. Trans. James Heisig and Paul Knitter. New York: Macmillan, 1988.

Fisher, Robert E. *Buddhist Art and Architecture*. London: Thames and Hudson, 1993.

Frederic, Louis. *Buddhism*. Flammarion Iconographic Guides. Paris: Flammarion, 1995.

Gross, Rita M. *Buddhism After Patriarchy: A Feminist History, Analysis, and Reconstruction of Buddhism*. Albany: State University of New York Press, 1993.

Kieschinck, John. *The Eminent Monk: Buddhist Ideals in Medieval Chinese Hagiography*. Honolulu: University of Hawaii Press, 1997.

LaFleur, William R. *Buddhism: A Cultural Perspective*. Englewood Cliffs, N.J.: Prentice Hall, 1988.

Mitchell, Donald W., and James Wiseman, eds. *The Gethsemani*

Encounter: A Dialogue on the Spiritual Life by Buddhist and Christian Monastics. New York: Continuum Publishing, 1997.

Nyanaponika, Thera, and Hellmuth Hecker. *Great Disciples of the Buddha*. Somerville, Mass.: Wisdom Publications, 1997.

Paul, Diana Y. *Women in Buddhism: Images of the Feminine in the Mahayana Tradition*. 2nd edition. Berkeley: University of California Press, 1985.

Perez-Remon, Joaquin. *Self and Non-self in Early Buddhism*. The Hague: Mouton, 1980.

Pilgrim, Richard B. *Buddhism and the Arts of Japan*. 2nd edition. Chambersburg, Pa.: Anima Books, 1993.

Prebish, Charles S. *American Buddhism*. Belmont, Calif.: Wadsworth Publishing, 1979.

Robinson, Richard H., and Willard L. Johnson. *Buddhism: A Historical Introduction*. 3rd Edition. Belmont, Calif.: Wadsworth Publishing, 1982.

Reat, Noble Ross. *Buddhism: A History*. Berkeley, Calif.: Asian Humanities Press, 1994.

Sadhatissa, H. *Buddhist Ethics: Essence of Buddhism*. New York: Braziller, 1970.

Snellgrove, David, ed. *The Image of the Buddha*. Paris: Unesco, 1978.

Strong, John S. *The Experience of Buddhism: Sources and Interpretations*. Belmont, Calif.: Wadsworth Publishing, 1995.

Suzuki, Daisetz T. *Zen and Japanese Culture*. Princeton: Princeton University Press, 1971.

Swearer, Donald K. *Buddhism and Society in Southeast Asia*. Chambersburg, Pa.: Anima Books, 1981.

Wriggins, Sally Hovey. *Xuanzang: A Buddhist Pilgrim on the Silk Road*. Boulder, Colo.: Westview Press, 1997.

Yin-Shun. *The Way to Buddhahood: Instructions from a Modern Chinese Master*. Somerville, Mass.: Wisdom Publications, 1998.

INDEX

(This index contains selected persons, places, events, and themes to help you find your way through the text. Numbers following entries indicate the *question* in which that entry is found.)